three ages of zen

of zen

Samurai, Feudal, and Modern

Published by The Buddhist Society
Patron: His Holiness the Dalai Lama
Registered Charity No. 1113705

First published by Charles E. Tuttle Publishing Co. 1993
Second edition published 1994
Third edition published by The Buddhist Society 2017
© Trevor Leggett Adhyatma Yoga Trust, 2017

Publication supported by The Trevor Leggett Adhyatma Yoga Trust.

ISBN: 978-0-901032-48-5 (The Buddhist Society)

A catalogue record for this book is available from the British Library

Note on illustrations: The author appreciates the contribution of the artist, Jacques Allais, to this book.

The character on the following page is MU, that state of no-thing-ness about which nothing can be said.

Edited by Sarah Auld
Designed by Avni Patel

Printed in Padstow, Cornwall by TJ International

The Buddhist Society
58 Eccleston Square
London
SW1V 1PH
T: 020 7834 5858
E: info@thebuddhistsociety.org
thebuddhistsociety.org

three ages of zen

of zen

Samurai, Feudal, and Modern

Trevor Leggett

Contents

THE TRANSLATIONS IN THIS TEXT ILLUSTRATE three phases of Zen in Japan: Warrior Zen of crisis, when Japan faced and repulsed Kublai Khan's naval attacks in the thirteenth century; feudal Zen for officials in the 250 largely peaceful years up to the Western naval attacks in the mid-eighteenth century; and twentieth-century Zen, before, through, and after World War II.

The three parts are concerned mainly with laymen's Zen. Mahayana Buddhism has always had a close connection with the world. It is indeed possible that it began with groups of laymen in India. In the first text, the warriors remained in fact laymen, taught mostly by monks. It is to be noted that some of them were women. There was no prejudice in Zen, as there sometimes was in other branches of Buddhism. But there were no concessions either.

The second part is an essay written for a samurai official by abbot Torei. Zen had fallen into decay and was being dramatically revived by Hakuin. It had to contend with government-sponsored Confucianism. That code, like the code of the gentleman, could become a cultivated semi-scepticism and end up as a shell of acceptable behaviour masking emptiness within.

The third part consists of extracts chosen by me from the published autobiography of Zen master Tsuji Somei (with his agreement). He did most of his training as a layman, becoming a priest relatively late in life. The account gives details of Zen practice in very severe conditions, when the author was a

prisoner of war in Siberia and other parts of Russia. (I should add that the heroism of Mrs. Tsuji, when left to bring up the family on her own, was of equal stature.)

Zen practice for laypeople in the world will be a more useful model for Westerners than monastery practice. There are some 15,000 temples in Japan but almost none in Western countries. Japanese monastery life is not feasible for people in the West, and in any case it has many elements which are not basic to Buddhism, but derive from Japanese customs. On the other hand, digging with a spade, or answering the telephone, or trying to settle a row are the same all over the world.

It has been one of the glories of Buddhism that besides living experience, it spreads compassion. For some 450 years up to the Mongol invasion, there was no death penalty in Japan; offenders were exiled to a small island. In some of the codes, torture was prohibited in cases short of murder; it was routine in most of Europe. On the cultural side, the technical vocabulary of most of the arts, including the so-called knightly arts, derives directly from Zen. Even in the most basic things, such as the 30% literacy rate in the middle ages, Japan stands out.

The inspirations arising from satori, or realization of truth, had to spread through lay-disciples such as those depicted here. There are areas such as present-day politics, where the inspirations have not been accepted. But Zen, or meditation (in Sanskrit, *dhyana*), has been a great light. As Torei remarks, one cannot do real good unless one can control one's own mind. Confucian and other morality, though it tells us what to do, does not show us how to control our minds so that we can do it.

Part One

Samurai Zen

THE ORIGIN OF WARRIOR ZEN IN KAMAKURA, and in the whole of the eastern part of Japan, goes back to the training of warrior pupils by Eisai (Senko Kokushi). But it was the training of warriors and priests by two great Chinese masters, Daikaku and Bukko, which became the Zen style of the Kamakura temples. There were three streams in Kamakura Zen: scriptural Zen, on-the-instant (*shikin*) Zen, and Zen adapted to the pupil (*ki-en* Zen).

Scriptural Zen derives from Eisai, founder of Jufukuji in Kamakura in 1215, and of Kenninji in Kyoto. But at that time it was rare to find any samurai who had literary attainments in Kamakura, so the classical koans from Chinese records of patriarchs could hardly be given to them. The teacher therefore selected passages from various sutras for the warriors, and for monks also. These specially devised scriptural Zen koans used by Eisai at Kamakura numbered only eighteen, and so the commentary to the Sorinzakki (Zen Analects) calls Jufukuji the Temple of the Eighteen Diamond Koans.

However, after Eisai, his successors of the Oryu line in Kamakura (to which he belonged – the founder died in China in 1069 and the line was dying out there when it was brought across by Eisai), soon brought them up to a hundred scriptural koans, to meet the various temperaments and attainments of their pupils. These successors were Gyoyu, Zoso, and Jakuan at Jufukuji; Daiei, Koho, and Myoo at Zenkoji; Sozan and Gakko at Manjuji, and others.

Among these augmented scriptural koans were passages from the sutras but also from the sayings of the patriarchs, to suit the depth or shallowness of comprehension of pupils, whether monks or laymen. Thus the warriors who applied for Zen training in Kamakura in the early days studied both the Buddha Zen (*nyorai* Zen) and the patriarchal Zen, but it can be said that those who were given classical koans from the *Hekiganshu* or the *Mumonkan* and so on would have been extremely few. From the end of the sixteenth century, however, the teachers did begin to rely mainly on stories from the records of the patriarchs for training both monks and laymen. Kamakura Zen gradually deteriorated, and by about 1630 no printed text of the *Shonankattoroku* existed, there were only manuscript copies. Sometime toward the end of the seventeenth century, a priest named Toan in Izumi selected ninety-five of the (Kamakura) scriptural koans, and got a friend, a priest named Soji, to have them printed as a two-volume work entitled *Kyojokoanshu* (Anthology of scriptural koans). These ninety-five correspond to the Kamakura scriptural koans, though with five missing (two from the Diamond Sutra, one from the Kegon Sutra, one from the Lotus Sutra, and one from the Heart Sutra). This book still existed in 1925.

On-the-instant Zen (*shikin*-Zen, sometimes read "sokkon-zen") arose from the training of warriors by Daikaku, first teacher at Kenchoji. He had come to Japan in 1246, and had stayed briefly at Enkakuji in Hakata City in Kyushu, and then at Kyoto; while his Japanese was still imperfect, and without taking time to improve it, he came to Kamakura. Thus this teacher had to be sparing of words, and in training students he did not present them with classical koans about Chinese patriarchs which would have required long explanations of the history and circumstances of the foreign country; instead he made koans then and there on the instant, and set them to the warriors as a means to give them the essential first glimpse. Bukko Kokushi, founder of Enkakuji, arriving in Japan on the last day of the sixth month of 1280, came to Kamakura in autumn of the same year, so that he too had no time to learn Japanese but began meeting people straight away. He also had to confine himself to speaking only as necessary, and in the same way made koans for his warrior pupils on the spur of the moment. Thus at both these great temples there was what was called *shikin*, or on-the-instant Zen. Before Daikaku came to Japan, something of the true patriarchal Zen had been introduced by such great Zen figures as Dogen and Shoichi (Bennen), but monks and laymen were mostly not equal to it and many missed the main point in a maze of words and phrases. Consequently Bukko finally gave up the use of classical koans for Zen aspirants who came to him in Kamakura, and made them absorb themselves in things directly concerning them. The regent Tokumine himself was one of the early pupils of this on-the-instant Zen, and he was the one who grasped its essence.

Zen adapted to the pupil meant, at Kamakura, making a koan out of some incident or circumstance with which a monk or layman was familiar, and putting forth test questions (*satsumon*) to wrestle with. It would have been very difficult for the Kamakura warriors, with their little learning, to throw themselves at the outset right into the old koan incidents in the records of the patriarchs. So in the

Zen temples of Kamakura and of eastern Japan generally, the style was that only when their Zen had progressed somewhat did they come under the hammer of one of the classical koans. Among the old manuscripts in the Kanazawa and Nirayama libraries there are many concerning Kamakura Zen, for instance *Nyudosanzenki* and *Gosannyudoshu*. But it is only the Shonankattoroku which is a commentary with details of when each koan began to be used as such, and in which temple, and also discourses and sermons on them. In the tenth month of 1543, a great Zen convention was held at Meigetsuin as part of the memorial service, on the 150th anniversary of the death of Lord Uesugi Norikata, its founder. Five hundred printed copies of the *Shonankattoroku* were distributed to those attending. The book included sermons on the koans by Muin, the *roshi* (aged priest) of Zenkoji. The work consisted of one hundred koan stories selected from *Gosannyudoshu* and other texts, by Muin Roshi, as particularly suited to the warriors whom he was training at the time. With the decline of Kamakura Zen at the end of the sixteenth century, the copies of this book disappeared and it became extremely difficult to find one. What remained in the temples were almost entirely manuscript copies.

In 1918 I examined the old records at Kenchoji in the four repositories of the sub-temples of Tengen, Ryuho, Hoju, and Sairai, and among the stacks of old books there were some seventeenth-century manuscript copies of the *Shonankattoroku*, but all had pages missing from the ravages of worms, and it was barely possible to confirm from part of the contents that they had all been copies of one and the same book. In the first years of Meiji, Yamaoka Tesshu was given a copy by the Zen priest Shojo of Ryutakuji in Izu, and he allowed Imai Kido to make a further copy of it.

In this way I came into touch with a copy, but this was lent and re-lent, and finally became impossible to trace. There are some collections of notes of laymen who were set some of these koans at Kamakura temples, but the teachers when they gave one did not say what number it was, and so in these notes the koans are not tabulated. It was only after finding a list of contents in one of the Kenchoji manuscripts that I was able to determine the order of the full one hundred koans as recorded in the present work. In Kamakura Zen there were thirty other koans used mainly by teachers of the Oryu line (mostly at Jufukuji, Zenkoji, and Manjuji – temples usually connected with Eisai), which are from *Bukedoshinshu* (thirteenth volume at Zenkoji), *Bushosodan* (eleventh volume at Jufukuji), and *Sorinzakki* (fifteenth volume at Kenchoji), but I have omitted these and present here only the hundred koans of Shonankattoroku.

Zen tests (*sassho*) differ with the teacher. Those given to those trained at Enkakuji in the Soryukutsu (Blue Dragon Cave) interview room of Master Kosen (one of the greatest Meiji roshis) were exceptional tests, and again the tests set by Shunno of Nanzenji and the formidable Sekisoken tests were not the same. The teachers Keichu and Shinjo had tests of their own. The *sassho* included here have been taken from a collection of 460 Kamakura *sassho* recorded in the *Tesshiroku* (fourth volume of the manuscript copy). These of course have themselves been picked out from many different interviews with different pupils, but I believe they would have been tests devised by teachers when each koan was first being set as such; so the collection will have come from over a hundred different teachers. Of course sometimes a single teacher devised more than one koan, but if we reckon that Kamakura teachers made 130 koans, we can take it that the *sassho* tests devised at the initiation of the separate koans would have come from over a hundred teachers.

The *Shonankattoroku* koans and sermons had discourses as well as a note as to the origination of each one, but here only this last is included. The discourses and sermons are so full of old Kamakura words and expressions that annotations would come to be as long as the original text.

Some tests require a "comment" (*chakugo* or *jakugo*). In general these are kept secret and not to be disclosed, but as an example I have included some of the comments on the Mirror Zen poems used at Tokeiji.

At the end of the sixteenth century Kamakura Zen was gradually deteriorating, and when with the Tokugawa period the country entered a long period of peace, warriors were no longer required to confront the issue of life and death on the battlefield. And it was perhaps for this reason that the quality of those who entered Kamakura Zen was not heroic like that of the old warriors, and both priests and lay followers became fewer. Kamakura Zen begins with "one word" and ends with absorption in "one Katzu!" Its main koan is the Katzu! and unless one could display Zen action at the turning point of life and death, he was not passed through. Sometimes a naked sword was at the centre of the interview (in later centuries the sword was represented by a fan).

Kamakura Zen was for those who might be called upon to die at any moment, and both teacher and pupils had to have tremendous spirit. Today those who with their feeble power of meditation casually entertain visions of passing through many koans cannot possibly undertake it. In that kind of Zen there were those who spent over ten long years to pass one single koan (for instance Tsuchiya Daian or Matsui Ryozen); how many years of painful struggle those like Kido took to pass through the "one word" koans of Kamakura Zen! These days people seem to expect to pass through dozens of koans in a year, and it cannot be called the same thing at all. Perhaps it might seem pointless to bring out this text now. After the passing of Master Shinjo, there are no more teachers who use Kamakura koans in their interviews, and again laymen who actually came under the hammer of this Zen now number only nine, all of them in their seventies or eighties. It is to prevent it from falling into untimely oblivion that I bring out this work, so that the fragments which Shunpo Roshi left shall not be entirely wasted. The old manuscripts stocked since 1919 in the Dokaiin repository of Kenchoji were taken out and aired on 1 September 1924, and in the Great Kanto Earthquake half of them were destroyed. The records of warrior Zen in particular, held under the collapsed building, became drenched with rainwater and entirely ruined. Thus it has become impossible to make a critical collation of the records, but fortunately from the hundreds of extracts already made and annotated over many years, it has been possible to investigate Kamakura Zen and to bring out this collection of one hundred koans properly edited. Some of the detail had to be determined by comparing as well as possible with what remained of the documents ruined by the earthquake, referring back also to the very many notes which I had myself taken earlier.

Since the earthquake, I have lived the Zen life, for a time in a retreat in Kyushu, and now buried in my books at Sofukuji. What remained from the earthquake has had to be left. But with my old, sick body it has been impossible to complete the full study of Kamakura Zen quickly, so first of all the full text of just the *Shonankattoroku* is to be brought out.

In the autumn of 1919 I received from Mr. Nakayama Takahisa (Ikkan) all the notes about warrior Zen left by the late Shunpo, roshi of Daitokuji, and to help me with these I examined the old records in the repositories of the Kamakura temples. At that time, thanks to the kindness of the *kancho* (superintendent priest) of Kenchoji, the old records of the Donge room were moved to the study in my lodgings there, so that I was able to examine the Zen records of old masters of many different periods. Again I must express gratitude for the cooperation of Zen master Kananawa, head of the sect administration, thanks to which my examination of documents and records from their stock of rare manuscripts was made so fruitful. Also I was permitted by the priests in charge to go over the records preserved in the repositories of Jufuku, Butsunichi, Garyu, and Hoju temples, which provided some precious material on old Zen. Now by good fortune the manuscript of *Shonankattoroku* is ready for publication, and I wish to set down my deepest gratitude and appreciation in regard to all those who have helped so much in the task.

IMAI FUKUZAN
Spring 1925

IN THE KYUDOSANZENKI (RECORDS OF LAY ZEN) – the postscript of the first volume of the manuscript of Zenko and the introduction to volume eight of the Kencho manuscripts – it is said that the Zen training of warriors at Kamakura fell into two stages. Up to the end of the Muromachi period (1568), incidents from the training of the earlier warrior disciples were set as koans to beginners, and only afterwards were the classical koans concerning Buddhas and patriarchs used extensively. The incidents from the Zen training of warriors were the kind recorded in the *Shonankattoroku*.

But after the end of the Muromachi period, it became common among teachers to present warriors with nothing but classical koans from the very beginning, and those who used the incidents from warrior training as koans gradually became very few, so that the three-hundred-odd koans which are known to have existed in Kamakura Zen came to be forgotten.

Among the teachers after Hakuin (died in 1768 at age eighty-four) there were still some who presented these incidents to pupils, but they were not set as koans to be wrestled with and answered in interviews with the teacher. There were some who, when a pupil stuck too long over one of the classical koans, brought out one of these old stories of the early samurai as a means to get him around the obstacle and bring him on to the right path from a new direction. In the interviews given by teachers of the Hakuin line, it can be said that no more than twelve or thirteen of the incidents from the training of warriors were known. Only in the Soryukutsu (Blue Dragon Cave) line were there still over a score of them in use.

However, teachers of the line from Kogetsu (died in 1751 aged eighty-five; founder of Fukujuji in Kurume, Kyushu) had a great deal to do with samurai, and in their interviews they preserved a tradition of this Zen, as suited to the inclination of their pupils. They used over one hundred such koans. The *Sorinzakki* (Zen Analects) and *Bukedoshinshu* (Records of Warriors Aspiring to the Way) list three hundred warrior koans, but in the Kogetsu tradition one who could pass through seventy-two of them was reckoned to have a complete mastery of all three hundred. In the interviews only 108 were being actually set as koans, and to solve the seventy-two main ones was to pass the whole collection. After the Meiji Restoration (1868) the last teachers to use them were Shinjo of the Hakuin line and Shunno of the Kogetsu line, and there were none who followed them in this so that at present (1920) there are no teachers who use them. Thus there are few today who know anything about the incidents recorded in the *Nyudosanzenki* and the other collections.

By the end of Muromachi the Kamakura koans were gradually being forgotten, and in the Zen which followed Hakuin they were almost entirely discarded. There was, however, still some tradition about them in Kyushu, and at the time of the Meiji Restoration Zen teachers all over the country were continually being asked about this Zen by samurai of the main Kyushu clans like Satsuma and Choshu. Many Rinzai teachers found they could not answer. However in the Soto line, Ekido the abbot of Sojiji, Kankei the abbot of Eiheiji, Bokusan of Kasuisai, and others knew warrior Zen well, and could meet the questions of the Kyushu civilians and warriors.

In the Rinzai line, there was an impression that samurai Zen had been Zen of repeating the name of Amida (*Nembutsu* Zen), and the teachers did not know about the Kamakura koans. Gyokai, abbot of Zojoji, of the Jodo sect, and Tetsujo, abbot of Chionin, as well as other spiritual leaders, of this line, taught samurai Zen as being Nembutsu, and often preached to the high officials and generals of those times. The teachers of other lines knew the stories, but simply related them and did not set them as koans to be wrestled with. In fact, what goes on in the interview room is different with each line, and is not something that should be spoken about lightly.

Warrior Zen began with the samurai who came to Eisai at Jufukuji in Kamakura, from 1215. (This temple burned down in 1247 and again in 1395, and many of the records were lost.) Historically this Zen was taught in the interviews of Rinzai masters, but now there are few within the Rinzai lines who know of it, though there are quite a few outside who have some knowledge. This is an ironic fact, on the discovery of which many inquirers into Zen have had to suppress a smile.

In the first years of Meiji, the Daikyoin in Tokyo began work examining old records in Zen temples, collaborating with some priests of the Rinzai line as well. (The Daikyoin was set up with some official support to advise on religious matters.) A glance at their bulletin makes the facts clear. Temples all over the country sent old records concerning warrior Zen to the Daikyoin for examination. The material was there classified under five headings: Zen connected with the Imperial Palace, shogun rulers, nobles, the gentry of various clans, and with simple warriors. Those parts which recorded koans were collated. This project was initiated at the suggestion of a monk named Taikoan. It was found that the Rinzai temples, obsessed with the principle of "no setting up of words," had not merely seen little necessity to keep records, but were very indifferent to the preservation of what records did exist. So there is very little material about what koans the teachers gave to the princes, nobles, warriors, and the ordinary people. Again, one incident which takes up five or six pages in records of the Soto and Obaku lines, in the Rinzai account may have barely half a page, so that sometimes it is quite difficult to make out all the main points. There are those who maintain that this is in accordance with the principle of directness, that "just one inch of the blade kills the man," but if this principle is applied to historical records, along with the other one of not setting up words in the first place, surely it is going too far.

Parts of the Daikyoin records have been damaged by insects and so on, but what follows is a list of the published collections of records which were then available to them.

The *Homeishu* (Record of the Cry of the Phoenix – in the records of Kenninji) and the *Undaigendan* (Discourses from the Cloud Dais – in the records of Nanzenji), in reporting the same incidents differ only in the length and detail of their accounts. Both of them begin with the interviews between the Empress Tachibana (Danrin), consort of Emperor Saga, and the Chinese Zen master Giku, about AD 815, and follow with an account of the interest taken in Zen by sixteen emperors, from Gotoba (1183–98) up to Go-mizuno-o (1611–29). Both of them have the imperial utterances expressed in classical *Yamatokotoba* (Yamato dialect), which are thus difficult to read without a translation into standard language. For this reason Shunpo himself had the idea that these are paraphrases of old court documents. However a copy in possession of Ekido of Sojiji was finally discovered which turned out to have these sections all transcribed into orthodox Chinese characters and thus easy to read.

Sorinzakki (Zen Analects) and a commentary on them were pieced together by Shunpo from various copies of parts of it which existed in the Kyoto temples, though owing to the fragmentary nature of the material he was never able to reconstruct a complete original text. In any case none of the Kyoto copies have anything before Onin (1467), and they stop at Genroku (1688), so they cannot be compared with the detailed historical accounts in the Kamakura records. The most complete version of the Sorinzakki and its commentary existed in Zenkoji in Kamakura, but even this goes no further than 1716 and can tell us nothing after that.

Bukedoshinshu (Records of Warriors Aspiring to the Way – no connection at all with the published book of the same name) is a collection of biographies of warriors who entered Zen training, took interviews with a teacher for some years, and were given a Zen name by the teacher when they had mastered the principle of Zen.

Bushosodan (Zen Stories of Warriors and Generals) and *Ryueizenna* (Zen Tales of Willow Camp) give accounts of Zen from the lives of generals from Hojo Tokiyori up to the Tokugawas. In the Jufukuji library these two have been bound together as an appendix to the *Bukedoshinshu*, with the title *Bumontetsuganzei* (Pupil of the Warrior Eye). This was written out by priest Gettei of the Jufukuji sub-temple Keikoan.

Nyudosanzenki (Accounts of Lay Zen) and *Gosannyudoshu* (Lay Training at Rinzai Temples) are accounts of training at the five temples of Kamakura.

Shonankattoroku (Record of Kamakura Koans) has one hundred koans consisting of incidents from the training of warriors.

Ka-an-zatsuroku (Analects of Ka-an) is a random collection of notes of incidents concerning the warriors, nobles, and officials who came from all over the country to priest Ka-an at Manjuji. At the beginning of the Meiji era many temples had manuscript copies of this, but now (1920) there is only one copy, consisting of twelve fascicles copied by Soku of Hokokuji.

Zendoguzuki (Record of the Propagation of Zen) begins with the meeting at Jufukuji between Eisai and Gyoyu, and gives further accounts of Zen training in Rinzai temples up to O-ei (1394). There is a manuscript copy in the library at Nirayama.

Zenjomonshokan (Mirror of Zen *Samadhi*) consists of biographies of warriors who trained under Zen teachers and finally received the full "approval" (*inka*) from them. This book extracts from the accounts in *Bukedoshinshu*, *Gosanyudoshu*, and others, those cases where the master finally gave approval to the pupil as having completed the training. This book was at Kanazawa before the partial dispersal of the library there, and is known to bibliophiles as an "ex-Kanazawa" book, as in the case also of *Shoinmanpitsu* (Jottings from the Shade of the Banana Tree), *Zenrinroeishu* (Zen Songs of Retainers), *Shochoshu* (Pine and Sea), *Towajusoshu* (Wind and Seaweed of Eastern Japan), *Sekirozakki* (Jottings from a Stone Hearth), *Shotoseigo* (Holy Words from Pine and Tide), *Fukugenrenpeki* (Wall around the Front of Bliss), *Hamanomezarashi* (Vision of the Beach), *Kaenshu* (Flowering Hedge Anthology), and others. All these record incidents of the warrior Zen tradition, and some of them also give poems which the warriors composed as answers to the koan tests. (This kind of answer is technically called *agyo*.)

In 1400 Zen master Daigaku Shuei made an examination of the Kanazawa library and cataloged the Zen manuscripts. Later Zenju, the 178th master of Kenchoji, when he became a teacher at Ashigaka College, examined the old manuscripts at Kanazawa and Nirayama libraries, and cataloged many hundreds of the old Zen records which he found there. The Zen teachers who were members of Daikyoin, in their search for accounts of warrior Zen, found and borrowed for examination many of the old manuscripts there through the librarian Suzuki Soei. The examination made it clear that the koans about which officials and warriors at the beginning of the Meiji era were asking Rinzai teachers were in fact very early incidents of the training of warriors by teachers of this same Rinzai sect.

No one can estimate how many hundreds and thousands of laypeople have practised Zen in Japan since the Empress Danrin at the beginning of the ninth century, and there must have been innumerable records of the koans set to them. The first time I saw any material on warrior Zen was in 1872 or 1873, when Zen master Bokusan presented my father with a notebook made by the Soto master Gattan, and a manuscript written by Zuiun of the Obaku sect. From these I got some idea of how teachers of Soto and Obaku used to handle their warrior pupils in the past. Then after attending the addresses given in Tokyo by Shunpo, roshi of Daitokuji, about the old records like *Bushosodan* and *Bukedoshinshu*, I discovered the still more drastic means which were used in the Rinzai sect for warriors. Later, Bairyo, kancho of Nanzenji, gave me copies of *Undaigendan*, *Homeishu* and other texts, from which I came to know about the direct Zen traditions which there had been at the Imperial Palace. Only after seeing the *Shonankattoroku* text which Yamaoka Tesshu had received from Shojo of Ryutaku temple in Izu did I first come to know that there had been a separate Zen tradition at Kamakura.

In 1872, Master Tekisui was elected General Head to represent the three Zen sects, and there were many laymen training in Zen. Master Shunpo too was active in the Daikyoin, and many leading figures in Zen were studying warrior Zen traditions; material about it was being collected in Tokyo so that there were good opportunities to study the koans of that tradition. But as in the case of the *Homeishu* text, where the Imperial utterances in the palace tradition were reported in *Yamatokotoba* (Yamato dialect), here too there was much use of classical Japanese words of antiquity, which could not be understood without a gloss in contemporary Japanese. In the Kamakura records again, there are many local words from several centuries in the past. To read the records themselves one has to peruse an old manuscript entitled *Old Deer Brush* by Master Sanpaku (156th master of Enkakuji), and then one has to know the obsolete words. Furthermore, the founders of all the Kamakura temples were Chinese of the Sung or Yuan dynasties, and in the old accounts there is much Chinese transcribed phonetically in a distorted way by writers who did not understand it. Without the glossary compiled by Ryuha, the 178th master of Kenchoji, there were many passages which could not be read, let alone understood. In an old Zenkoji record (which was still preserved in Jufukuji around 1868) there is a report of a meeting between Hojo Tokimune and Bukko Kokushi, and in it comes this: "*kun-sun-rii, kun-sun-rii, raunau, ya-shi-yan-kin-gu-a.*" Today there is hardly a soul who could read this and understand it. It was always supposed that it must have been some koan. Around 1873, when there were many great figures of Zen coming and going around the Daikyoin, there was no one, not even Shunpo Roshi, who was consultant professor to the three head temples Daitokuji, Myoshinji, and Kenninji, who could suggest any meaning for this Sung Chinese which Bukko spoke to Tokimune. Nobody had any idea what it was. But when the glossary of Ryuha was acquired by the Daikyoin, the passage "kun-sun-rii... " turned out surprisingly to be "Come in! Come in! I have something to say to Your Honour." This caused general laughter. In the Kamakura records there are many similar old records of Sung Chinese transcribed phonetically. So there are many inconveniences in the study of Zen there. But after being presented with the *Reikenroku* (Record of the Spiritual Sword – the copy in the Butsunichian is called *Jintoroku*) with the red-ink notes by Kaigan Roshi and textual amendments by Tokoku Roshi, I found that the bulk of the three hundred warrior koans recorded in the *Sorinzakki* and elsewhere were Kamakura Zen.

For his research on old Kamakura Zen, Shunpo made notes on the backs of used pieces of paper. (He almost never used a clean sheet, but always the backs of pieces of wrapping paper and so on. The only time he used a new sheet of paper was for a final fair copy.) Before he could collate all his material into a text, he had to return to Kyoto in 1875, on account of urgent affairs connected with the administration of the colleges attached to the great temples there – so I heard indirectly from others. No one else who had been studying warrior Zen had completed any of the drafts either, and finally it was left to the general research council of ten Zen temples (I recall that this was founded in 1875), which entrusted it to Imagita Kosen Roshi. At that time, however, he was himself engaged in many projects, and from Enkakuji was promoting Zen vigorously in the Kanto area. He became head of the seven lines of the Rinzai sect, and with all his administrative engagements had no time to examine ancient records. He therefore divided the task among the many laymen who were training under him.

Ichinyo (Miyata Chuyu), Ryumon (Hirata Yasumaru), and others examined the records of Zen at the palace; Mumon (Oi Kiyomichi), Rakuzan (Suzuki Yoshitaka), and others took the documents on shogun Zen; Ryozen (Ishii Tokihisa), Katei (Yamada Toshiaki), and others studied warrior Zen; Daian and Kido worked solely on Kamakura Zen. But many of them had official duties and little time for the research, and if they were sent abroad it had to be

THREE AGES OF ZEN

set aside. Moreover, those officials in the ministries of education and the army who had given support around 1878 were completely occupied with their responsibilities when the Satsuma rebellion broke out, and had no opportunity for anything else. Senior men like Otori Keisuke and Soejima had to carry out diplomatic missions abroad, and the interest in warrior Zen slipped into the background. After the death of Yamaoka Tesshu in 1889, those who could say anything on this kind of Zen gradually became few; Katsu Kaishu, Takahashi Deishu, Shimao Tokuan, and other great Zen laymen died, and almost no one knew anything about the subject. While the Daikyoin existed in Tokyo there were a good many among the Zen teachers who knew about this laymen's Zen, and there were many who used Zen stories of the warriors. As we can see from their recorded sermons, Masters Dokuan and Keichu were speaking on palace Zen, Mugaku, Teizan, and Shunpo on warrior Zen in general, and Kosen and Shinjo on Kamakura Zen in particular. But as there was nobody who could present Kamakura Zen apart from the dozen koans which were given in interviews, teachers who had not seen texts like the *Sorinzakki* and its commentary tended to think that Kamakura Zen was nothing more than these dozen koans – perhaps to the quiet amusement of men like Tesshu and Kaishu. But Shunpo Roshi, on the other hand, had heard the discourses of Master Myoho of Hofukuji (at Iyama in Bicchu) on the *Bukedoshinshu*, *Reikenroku*, *Bushosodan*, and so on, and knew well about the Kamakura koans, information which he transmitted to admirers in Tokyo; those who wanted warrior Zen called him Prince of Teachers.

In 1875 he left Tokyo and in March two years later passed away in Kyoto. It is just fifty years since his death, and there are only nine people left in Tokyo who came in touch with his greatness, all of them fine, vigorous old men. Talking to them about the teacher and about Kamakura Zen, one has a strong feeling about how Zen has changed. For the fiftieth anniversary in March this year, Zen master Nyoishitsu of Kofukuji desires to distribute some work of Shunpo as a "fan for the eternal breeze of the Way." But the only draft which the teacher left was one called *Shokaigifu* (Voyager on the Ocean of the Absolute), which was not concerned with warrior Zen, and all the rest was no more than notes.

When I looked through these notes and fragments formerly, I noticed that a great number were concerned with Kamakura Zen; but to arrange these miscellaneous scraps written on the backs of used pieces of paper into a connected text was not something that could be done in a hurry. It would have been impossible, with the limitations imposed by the publication plan, to write up everything connected with Kamakura Zen. So it came about that Master Nyoishitsu began to press for the publication, on the fiftieth anniversary, of the first part only. This was to be an edited and supplemented edition of the *Shonankattoroku*.

The whole work projected is to be called *Bushizenkienshu* (Records of Warrior Zen Training) and the present text is to be just a first part. I have been told that there are 3,600 pages about warrior Zen in existence, bound into thirty-six volumes of a hundred pages each, which have been produced by laymen under the direction of great Zen teachers. And I have wondered whether it might be possible to put them into permanent form. With the loss of so many of the old manuscripts in the Great Kanto Earthquake, it is not feasible to collect and collate all the material in a short time. All I can hope is that one day I shall complete the work on warrior Zen, of which this *Shonankattoroku* is to be the first part. I am a retired scholar already over seventy, and writing is more and more a burden. But I have a dharma link with my old teacher Shunpo, whose discourses I so often attended, and I rejoice that the draft of the work has been completed for publication on the fiftieth anniversary of his passing. I beg the indulgence of readers for faults they may find in it.

The Warrior Koans*

*The following koans have been selected from the original text; the numbers given correspond to those in the original translation. The full translation of the remaining Kamakura koans with an index of the Chinese characters can be found in *Samurai Zen – The Warrior Koans*, translated by Trevor Leggett, Routledge, 2002.

NO. 1 *The mirror of Engakuji*

Regent Tokiyori founded the great temple of Kenchoji for the teaching of Buddhism, but the temple soon could not accommodate all the many warriors who became students (*nyudo*) in order to enter the Buddhist path and give all their free time to it. So in the first year of Koan (1278) Tokimune, Tokiyori's son, decided to build another great temple, and invited priest Rankei (afterwards Daikaku) to choose the Brahma-ground, as the site for a temple is called. Teacher and regent walked together around the nearby hills, and found the ruins of a Shingon temple (of the Mantra sect) where Minamoto Yoshiyori had once set up a Pagoda of Perfect Realization. They decided on this as the place to plant the banner of the Law.

First the teacher performed a purification, and made three strokes with a mattock; then the regent made three strokes, and planted a stalk of grass to mark the spirit of faith.

In the winter of the same year, when Tokimune was having the area prepared for the foundations, a buried stone coffer was found. In it was a perfect circular mirror; engraved on the back were the words EN KAKU – perfect realization. So the temple was called Enkakuji, or Engakuji.

Taira Masatsuna, a *nyudo* student of Zen (later Bukko), told him this story of how the temple came to be called Engakuji at an interview with Mugaku. The teacher said: "Leave for a moment that perfect mirror buried underground: the perfect mirror at this instant in your hands, what is it? Try and bring it out of its stone coffer. If you don't get this, the Spiritual Pagoda of Perfect Realization will not be built."

TESTS

1. When the stone coffer is broken open, what is that perfect mirror like?

Imai's note: It is said that this question means, When man dies, what happens to his spirit?

2. Beneath the feet of the man of the Way, as he walks, is the Brahma-ground for the temple. At this instant, try building the pagoda of Perfect Realization.

This incident became a koan in Kamakura Zen at the interviews of Butsuju, the 21st teacher at Engakuji.

NO. 3 *Saving Kajiwara's soul*

On the fifteenth day of the seventh month of the sixth year of Kencho (1255), the rite of Feeding the Hungry Ghosts was being performed at the Karataka mountain gate of Kenchoji temple. When the sutra reading had been completed, however, priest Rankei (Master Daikaku) suddenly pointed to the main gate and shouted: "A knight has come through the gate. It is Kajiwara Kagetoki, of many treacheries. Bring him to salvation quickly!"

The monks all stared hard at the gate, but could see no knight there. Only the head monk shouted, "Clear to see!" He left the line and went back to the Zen hall.

The teacher berated the others, saying: "Look at the crowds of you, supposed to be saving myriad spirits in the three worlds, and yet you cannot save one knight – blind clods! The rite must be performed again at the main gate, and the Heart Sutra recited in its original Sanskrit."

So the whole ceremony was transferred from the mountain gate to the main gate, and the sutra was recited there in Sanskrit.

After the recitation was over, the monks hurried to the Zen hall and asked the head monk, "How did you see the knight?"

He replied: "With the eye of the crown of the head, bright and clear!"

TESTS

1. Put aside for the moment the question of Kajiwara Kagetoki's apparition at Kenchoji, do you see the knight galloping his horse across the garden to the interview room here? If you can, save him quickly!

2. What was the virtue of chanting the sutra in Sanskrit at the main gate? Say!

Imai's note: The point of this second test is, Can chanting the Sutra in Sanskrit bring salvation to Kajiwara, or can it not? He who says that it can, will have to come under the teacher's hammer yet again. Until one has passed this koan, his reading of the sutras, whether as monk or layman, is equally meaningless. The koan must not be taken lightly.

This first became a koan in Kamakura Zen at the interviews of Daisetsu, the 47th master of Kenchoji.

NO. 5 *Bukko's one-word sutra*

Ryo-A, a priest of the Tsurugaoka Hachiman Shrine, came to Magaku (National Teacher Bukko, who succeeded Daikaku), and told him the story of Daikaku's one-word sutra. He said: "I do not ask about the six or seven syllables recited by other sects, but what is the one word of Zen?"

The teacher said: "Our school does not set up any word, its dharma is a special transmission outside of scriptures, a truth transmitted from heart to heart. If you can penetrate through to that, your whole life will be a *dharani* (Buddhist mantra), and your death will be a *dharani*. What would you be wanting with a word or half a word? The old master Daikaku went deep into the forest and put *one word* down there, and now the whole Zen world is tearing itself to pieces on the thorns, trying to find it. If the reverend Ryo-A before me wishes to grasp that one word, then without opening the mouth, do you recite the sutra of no-word. If you fail in your awareness of the no-word, you will at once lose the one word. Displayed, the one word is set above the thirty-three heavens; buried, it is at the bottom of the eighth great hell. Yet in all four directions and above and below, where could it ever be hidden? At this instant before your reverence! Is there a word, or is there not?"

The golden needle did not penetrate (the embroidered cloth of the priest's mind), and he left silently.

TEST

Say a word for the priest.

This incident became a koan in Kamakura Zen at the interviews of Gyokkei, the 131st master at Engakuji.

NO. 7 *The bucket without a bottom*

Imai's note: The nun Mujaku, whose lay name was Chiyono, was a woman of Akita who married and had one daughter. In 1276, when she was thirty-four, her husband died, and she could not get over the grief. She became a nun, and trained under Bukko. The story is that on the evening of a fifteenth day of August, when she was filling her lacquer flower-bucket where the valley stream comes down, the bottom fell out; seeing the water spilling she had a flash of insight, and made a poem on it to present to the teacher. Later he set her a classical koan, Three pivot-phrases of Oryu, and examined her minutely on it, and she was able to meet the questions. Again she continued interviews with him for a long time, and in the end he "passed over the robe and bowl," namely, authorised her as a successor to teach. Uesugi, Nikaido, and others had built Keiaiji temple in Kyoto, and asked her to become the first teacher there. It was not unusual in Zen for a teacher to be a woman.

After Bukko died, a hermitage called Shomyakuan was built for her at Shirogita to be the temple of Bukko's grave. She died in November 1298 at the age of seventy-six. [There is some discrepancy in the dates.—Tr.]

Mujaku, whose lay name was Chiyono, came to Bukko, Teacher of the Nation, and said, "What is Zen?"

The teacher said, "The heart of the one who asks is Zen; it is not to be got from the words of someone else."

The nun said, "Then what is the teacher doing, that he gives sermons and they are recorded?"

Imai's note: Bukko's Japanese being inadequate, he gave his sermons in Sung dynasty Chinese; they were recorded and later translated, then distributed to his Japanese followers. This is what the nun is referring to.

The teacher said, "To a deaf man, you show the moon by pointing; to a blind man, you show the gate by knocking on it with a tile."

Just then one of the deer near the Hakugando Stream gave a cry. The teacher said, "Where is that deer?"

The nun listened. The teacher gave a Katzu! shout and said: "Who is this listening?"

At these words the nun had a flash of illumination, and went out. At the water pipe from the Hakugando she took up a lacquered wooden bucket for flowers. As she was holding it full of water, she saw the moon's reflection in it, and made a poem, which was presented to the teacher:

> The flower bucket took the stream water and held it,
> And the reflection of the moon through pines lodged
> there in purity.

Bukko could not understand the poem in Japanese, so priest Gio translated it into Chinese and showed it to him. Bukko glanced at it and said "Nun, take the *Heart Sutra* and go."

After that, she had interviews with the master, coming and being sent away. In the end the lacquer bucket broke, and she presented another poem, of this realization:

The bottom fell out of Chiyono's bucket;
Now it holds no water, nor does the moon lodge there.

Imai's note: The account in *Zenmonkaikiden* says Chance or design? The bottom fell out of her bucket; Now it holds no water, nor does the moon lodge there.

After Chiyono's death the nun Nyozen of Tokeiji used to meditate on this poem as her basic theme. Nyozen's lay name was Takihime (or Takkino, according to the account in the *Bukedoshinshu*—Imai), and she had been of the household of Oi Toshiharu, a retainer of the Uesugi family. She trained under Geno, the founder of Kaizoji, and in 1313 she grasped the essence of Zen, presenting this poem to her teacher:

The bottom fell out of the bucket of that woman of humble birth;
The pale moon of dawn is caught in the rain puddles.

TESTS

1. What does the poem about the water from the water pipe caught in the bucket really mean?

2. What really is the bucket without a bottom?

3. What is the real meaning of the poem of the nun of Nyozen?

These poems were used as koans at Engakuji itself after the time of Daiko, the 5th teacher at the beginning of the Shoan era (1299).

Imai's note: From the Bunroku era (1592), what was called *Heart sutra* Zen became fashionable in Kamakura: a *chakugo* comment had to be found to fit certain phrases of the sutra. The poems of the two nuns came to be used as comments, so a further test came into existence:

4. What are the phrases from the *Heart Sutra* to fit the poems of the nuns? Say!

NO. 8 *Jizo stands up*

When Hojo Soun attacked Odawara castle and was occupying Kanto, the eastern part of Japan, the soldiers of the areas around Kamakura forced their way onto the lands of the temples; as their number gradually increased, Kenchoji was in dire straits.

On a winter day in the first year of Tenmon (1532), the teacher Yakkoku, the 169th master at Kenchoji, disregarding his own illness got up and gave an address from the high seat. Glaring at the congregation, of all ranks, he said:

"Men of great virtue, I ask you this – make the seated Jizo image in this hall stand up!"

Out of this occasion came one of the koans at Kenchoji. The samurai Mamiya Munekatsu, who had a position as a temple official, confined himself in the great hall where the image was a wooden Jizo seated on the lotus altar – for forty-one days, vowing to make the Jizo stand up. He was continuously reciting the mantra of Jizo: OM! KA-KA-KA! BISANMAYE SOWAKA! [This approximates the Sanskrit which glorifies Ksitigarbha as the Smiling One; Ka-ka-ka! represents a great laugh—Tr.] On the last night of the vow he was running around the hall like a madman, shouting "Holy Jizo, stand up!" At two o'clock in the morning the monk who was making the rounds struck the regulation single blow on the sounding board which hangs in front of the hall.

Munekatsu suddenly had a realization, and cried:

"Holy Jizo – it's not that he stands up, and it's not that he sits down. He has a life which is neither standing nor sitting."

TESTS

    1. See how you can get the sitting Jizo to stand up.

    2. See how you can get the standing Jizo to sit down.

    3. What is the life of the Jizo besides standing or sitting? Say!

This became one of the Kamakura koans at the interviews of Ryoko when he was the 172nd master at Kenchoji.

NO. 17 *Numbering the waves on Yui beach*

Minamoto Munatsune, in the spring of the first year of Shogen (1259) when he was seventy-five years of age, came to Kenchoji with the name of Gido to become a shaven-headed monk. The great teacher Rankei (namely Daikaku) had an informal interview with him, and taking him to be good spiritual material, set him the riddle of how many waves there are on Yui beach.

Gido poured out his heart's blood on this for two years, and finally, breaking through the confusion, he made answer in a Chinese poem:

On the ocean of the holy dharma
There is neither movement nor stillness.
The essence of the wave is like a mirror;
When something comes, the reflection appears.
When there is nothing in the mind,
Wind and waves are both forgotten.

He made a verse in Japanese about his time of practice:

Two years of wandering on Yui beach
There was no need to number off the waves.

TESTS

1. Count the waves on Yui beach.

2. What has Gido's verse about the ocean of the holy dharma got to do with how many waves there are? Say!

3. What does Gido's Japanese verse mean?

This incident became a koan in Kamakura Zen at the interviews given by Ikka, the 145th master at Kenchoji.

Imai's note: There are some at the present time who take this koan of the number of waves at Yui beach as the same as the number of hairs on the head, which is given in Hakuin's line. But they derive from different traditions. The koan "How many hairs are there on your head?" which is used as a test (*sassho*) comes from a phrase of Gyozan, whereas the question about the number of waves at Yui, when used in Kamakura Zen as relating to some words of Oryu, is not to be understood in the same way. Its ultimate meaning can be found when the eye is opened under the stick of the master.

NO. 18 *Tokimune's thing below the navel*

[When Tokimune received the news that the Mongol Armada was poised to attack Japan, he went in full armour to see Bukko his teacher and said, "The great thing has come," to which the teacher replied, "Can you somehow avoid it?" Tokimune calmly stamped his feet, shook his whole body, and gave a tremendous shout of Katzu! The teacher said: "A real lion cub, a real lion roar. Dash straight forward and don't look around!" After the defeat of the Mongols, Tokimune built the great monastery of Engakuji, and installed in it the representation of Jizo-of-a-thousand-forms. Bukko became the first teacher there. Tokimune arranged a great service for the souls of the dead of both sides. Soon afterward he died at the age of thirty-three. In the funeral oration Bukko said that he had been a bodhisattva – "for nearly twenty years he ruled without showing joy or anger; when the victory came he showed no elation; he sought for the truth of Zen and found it."—Tr.]

At the outbreak of war in the first year of Koan (1278) Tokimune visited Bukko and gave the Katzu! shout of dashing straight forward. Priest Gio said: "The general has got something great below his navel, so the shout too is great."

The field of the Elixir (*tanden*, the energy centre an inch below the navel) of Taoist doctrine was called *shii-ku-ii-mo* in Szechuan dialect, or "the thing under the navel." Gio was a priest from Szechuan who had come from Daikaku to Kenchoji in Japan, and in praising the greatness of Hojo Tokimune's *tanden* energy, he used this Szechuan phrase. [Like many remarks of the Chinese, it was transcribed into Chinese characters, and the Japanese, not knowing the Szechuan phrase, took it in the literal sense—Tr.]

One of the regent's ministers, Masanori, when he came to know what Gio had said, asked him indignantly:

"When did Your Reverence see the size of what the lord has below his navel?"

The priest said, "Before the general was born, I saw it."

The courtier did not understand.

The priest said, "If you do not understand the greatness of what is below the general's navel, then see through to before you yourself were born, the greatness of the thing below the navel. How would that thing become greater or less by the honour or contempt of high or low?"

The courtier was still more bewildered.

The priest gave a Katzu! shout and said, "Such is the voice of it, of that thing."

At these words the courtier had an insight and said, "This petty official today has been fortunate enough to receive a Katzu! from you. I have known the greatness of that thing below our lord's navel."

The priest said, "What is its length and breadth, say!" The courtier said, "Its length pierces the three worlds, its breadth pervades all ten directions."

The priest said: "Let the noble officer present a Katzu! of that greatness to show the proof."

The courtier was not able to open his mouth.

TESTS

1. What is the meaning of dashing straight ahead?

2. Say directly, what is the general's dashing straight forward.

3. Leaving the general's dashing straight forward, what is your dashing straight forward, here and now? Speak!

4. Leaving your dashing straight forward, what is the dashing straight forward of all the Buddhas and beings of the three worlds?

5. Leaving the dashing straight forward of the Buddhas and beings, what is the dashing straight forward of heaven and earth and the ten thousand phenomena?

6. Leaving for the moment the thing below the navel of the Taoists, what is the thing below the navel in our tradition? Say!

7. Say something about the thing below the navel before father and mother were born.

8. When the light of life has failed, say something about that thing below the navel.

9. Leaving the general's Katzu! – when you yourself are threatened by an enemy from somewhere, what great deed will you perform? Say!

10. Give a Katzu! for the courtier to prove it.

This became a koan when Torin, 44th master of Kenchoji, began to use it in interviews.

Imai's note: According to the records in Gosannyudoshu in Kamakura the samurai there were set this koan and wrestled with it, and even after "seeing the nature" they were never passed through it for at least five or six years. It is said that "dash straight forward" in the first tests was often taken as meaning "swiftly" or "sincerely," and that these were never passed.

NO. 22 *Stopping the fighting across the river*

In the first year of Te Yu (1275) priest Mugaku (Bukko) had planted the banner of the dharma at Chenju temple in the province of T'ai Chou when the Mongols invaded China and overran the province. The teacher withdrew to Nengjen temple in Wen Chou, but the next year they plundered that province, too. When one party of Mongol soldiers attacked Nengjen temple, everyone fled except the teacher, who sat quietly in the main hall.

(The official) Ch'en Kuo-hsiang often visited the master as a pupil. The teacher, pointing to the Mongol camp across the river, said, "There is a rope across the river into the camp. Do you make trial of it." (Do you stop the fighting—Imai.)

Hsiang said, "How can I make trial of it?"

The teacher suddenly grabbed hold of Hsiang and slapped his face. Hsiang instantly had a realization, and made a bow.

TEST

How can a slap be instant realization?

This was first used as a koan subject in the interviews of Sei Seccho.

NO. 24 *The Cave of Man in Mount Fuji*

Imai's Note: In the *Record of Nine Generations of the Hojo Rulers*, the first part, the following story occurs:

On the third day of the sixth month of the third year of Kennin (1203) the Shogun Yoriie went hunting on the foot-slopes of Mount Fuji, in the country of Suruga. There is a big cave on the lower slope of the mountain which the local people call the Cave of Man. He thought he would like to find out where it led, and called Nitta Shiro Tadatsune; giving him a most precious sword, he told him to go into the cave and explore it to the end. Tadatsune bowed, received the sword, and withdrew. At the head of a party of six, he went into the cave. The next day, the fourth, at the hour of the snake (10 a.m.) Shiro Tadatsune came back out of the cave, his journey altogether having taken a day and a night. He was brought before the shogun to report, and this was his account:

The cave became very narrow so that it was difficult even to turn around; they had to squeeze through one after another, and as in a nightmare they felt they could hardly move. The darkness was indescribable. The party had a pine torch each, they kept in touch by calling to each other. A stream running along the bottom soaked their feet. Innumerable bats, startled by the lights, flew on ahead, filling the passage. They were black like the ordinary bat, but with not a few white ones among them. As they followed the stream, little snakes were continuously coiling themselves around their feet; they had to keep cutting and cutting into the stream to get to these, in order to get on. Sometimes a rank smell of raw flesh assailed their nostrils and at times they felt sick, but again a delicious, heart-soothing fragrance would also come.

The passage gradually widened, and above them something like a transparent column, as it were a pillar of blue ice, was clearly seen. One of the men said that he had heard this kind of stalactite was a mineral from which the Sennin immortals prepare the nectar of immortality – so he had been told.

As they went further, under their feet came the thunder of furious shouts as from a thousand throats of demons fighting. It was terrifying.

Going still further they lit more pine torches, and saw that the place had widened out somewhat. On every side they could see nothing but pitch-black emptiness, but from time to time, human cries from far and near arose. Their hearts contracted as at treading the paths of hell.

Now they came to a wide river. There was no indication of the way (no "miyako-bird"—allusion to Narihira's famous poem). By the sound of it, a torrent was running down into an unimaginable abyss. They tested the surging current with their feet, and it was swift as an arrow and colder than any ice – as if it were from the frozen hells Guren and Daiguren.

The further bank was 200 to 250 feet away, and opposite them there appeared a light that was something like a blazing torch but not the colour of fire; in the light they described an awe-inspiring form standing in majesty.

Four of the men fell dead then and there. Tadatsune bowed to that spirit, and hearing its voice inwardly, threw the precious sword into the river, upon which the wonderful form disappeared and Tadatsune, his life spared, returned and gave his account.

Shogun Yoriie, hearing thus about the world within different from this world, determined to send another expedition with many men and a specially made boat.

But his senior counsellors dissuaded him, telling him that according to tradition this cave was the abode of the great Bodhisattva of Asama, and from ancient times men had not been permitted to look upon it.

The *nyudo* Wada Hidetsura, going to Kenchoji for an interview with Master Nanzan (the 20th teacher there), asked about this story of the Cave of Man in the field at the foot of Mount Fuji. The priest said: "What your honour has related is a tale of the heroic daring of warriors. The heroism in Zen must be of penetrating to the uttermost depths of the Cave of Man.

"When the aspirant begins his training and enters the Cave of Man in the Field of Zen, as he goes further in, he gets a feeling of his feet being cut by icy waters. He experiences sensations of fragrance, and then again there are perceptions of bright light. The treasure sword which he received from his master – there comes a time when he throws it away. When he throws it away, the form of the spirit, which he has been seeing, suddenly vanishes. While yet he sees this spirit form, he is caught by the Buddha, tied up by the dharma, and cannot have the freedom of Zen inspiration. But after the spirit form vanishes, he must go yet one more step into the interior. Do you not hear what I am saying? If you want to have the full view of a thousand miles, mount one more story of the tower."

TESTS

1. Going into the Zen cave, there is a feeling of the feet being cut by icy water. Why is that?

2. Why do sensations appear like a bad smell or a fragrance?

3. When comes the awareness of bright light?

4. What is the throwing away of the precious sword?

5. What is the appearance of the spirit form?

6. After the spirit form disappears, what is there further within?

Imai's note: The *Bushosodan* records that these tests were used in the interviews of warriors when Kosen Ingen (38th master at Kenchoji) was teaching at Chojuji in Kamakura. They were used when aspirants were entering on the practice of Zen meditation. But in times like the present (1925), when the importance of Zen meditation is overlooked, there will be few who could answer them properly. The fashion of Zen these days, among monks and laymen alike, is to absorb oneself in examining the words of the patriarchs in the koans, and since they do not experience the states of Zen meditation, there are hardly any who could open their mouths to these tests. The tests have as subject the meditation experiences of a Zen aspirant, experiences of the Six Consciousnesses (senses plus mind), then making void the Seventh Consciousness, and then thrusting a sword down into the heart-field of the Eighth *alaya* Consciousness. When as at present "philosophical" followers of Zen hope to travel the path of the patriarchs at high speed, on an express train as it were, these koans are quite unsuitable for them. But twenty or thirty years ago, among some of the senior laymen who practised Zen, there were quite a few who actually went through them.

NO. 28 *The rite of the wind god at Kamakura*

In the second year of Kangi (1229) there were portents of evil in the east of Japan. On the sixth day of the seventh month there was a frost at Kamakura, and at the Kanago district in Musashi province, flakes of snow fell. The diviners searched the records, to find that in the thirty-ninth year of the reign of the Emperor Kogen (reigned 214–148 BC) snow had fallen in the sixth month, and there had been a great snowfall in the sixth month of the thirty-fourth year of the Empress Suiko (AD 592–628), and another in the same month of the eighth year of the era called Engi (the middle part of the reign) of Emperor Daigo (AD 897–930). At these times there had been a bad year, the people in distress and fighting breaking out between local gangs. The diviners gave grave warnings that the omens portended calamities of a similar nature, with starvation and insurrection. Hojo Yasutoki was deeply disturbed. Then an official messenger from Mino brought a report from headman Makida that a sudden and intense fall had covered the ground in snow more than a foot deep.

At this Yasutoki was still more anxious, and he had prayers said in the great temples to avert disaster, but to no avail, for the next year in the fifth month, storms and floods continued for several weeks, and the whole land and everything in it was in dire straits. Yasutoki now had the esoteric ceremonies for salvation in crisis performed at all temples, and had the *Heart Sutra* read continuously by the priests at Tsurugaoka Hachiman Shrine. But the force of the wind did not abate.

Then he proposed to perform a sacrificial rite to the wind god at the stone torii at Yui-ura; he put the magistrate Yasusada in charge, and to help him ordered the priest Gyoyu (the 2nd master of Jufukuji, and also an expert in the esoteric Shingon ceremonies, of which he had been a priest before he entered Zen) to put together a text for the rite.

It happened that Enni Joza (Zen master Shoichi) was staying temporarily and teaching Zen at the small temple Zokyoin within the Jufukuji compound, and he was famous for his Chinese learning. Gyoyu therefore asked him whether he would do it, to which he at once agreed, and taking up the brush, wrote:

> All things are passing,
> Their nature is to arise and end;
> When arising and ending come to an end,
> That Nirvana is bliss.

Gyoyu looked at this and said doubtfully, "But this is the verse from the funeral service!"

Enni said, "We want to have a funeral for the wind devil. Why should we just imitate others when we compose the text for the rite?"

Then Gyoyu and Enni went together, and on the dais of the rite of the wind god, they recited the funeral verse. It is said that the wind immediately changed and dropped.

This is an old Zen story, to engage the idle moment. It is easily misunderstood. Right now, here in these Jewel Deer hills, hurricanes and floods are rising, and our Engakuji here is on the verge of being overwhelmed! I have to perform the rite of the wind god. Let each one of you bring me a verse with which I can give a funeral to the wind devil.

TESTS

1. Where does the wind arise from? Say!
2. Where does the wind devil live? Say!
3. What does the wind devil look like?
4. After the funeral, where does the wind devil go back to? Say!
5. Give me a funeral verse – compose it now!

This first became a Kamakura koan at the interviews of Kosan, the 29th teacher at Engakuji.

NO. 33 *The cat monster*

When Odawara castle fell to the attackers in the Meio period (the end of the fifteenth century), Akiko, who had been a maid in the service of Mori Fujiyori, the lord of the castle, escaped with a cat which had been her pet for many years. She took refuge in the village of the painter Takuma at Kinokubo by the Nameri River. She had been living for some years when the cat became a wild supernatural monster which terrorised the people, finally even preying on infants in the village.

The local officials joined with the people in attempts to catch it, but with its strange powers of appearing and disappearing, the swordsmen and archers could find nothing to attack, and men and women went in dread day and night.

Then in the twelfth month of the second year of Eisho (1505), priest Yakoku went up on to the dais at Hokokuji and drew the picture of a cat, which he displayed to the congregation with the words: "As I have drawn it, so I kill it with a Katzu!, that the fears may be removed from the hearts of the people." After this he gave the Katzu! shout, and tore the picture of the cat to pieces.

On that day, a woodcutter in the valley near the Takuma villa heard a terrible screech; he guided a company of archers to the upper part of the valley, where they found the body of the cat-monster, as big as a bear cub, dead on a rock. The people agreed that this had been the result of the master's Katzu!

1. How can tearing up a picture with a Katzu! destroy a living monster?

2. That devil-cat is now rampaging among the people, bewitching and killing them. Kill it quickly with a Katzu! Show the proof!

Imai's note: This is an exercise in the Katzu!

NO. 36 *Yakushi of a thousand forms*

On the eighth day of the eleventh month of the first year of Katei (1235), General Yoritsune was in great pain from an infected wound. All shrines and temples were to offer prayers for him, and the Buddhist image-maker Yasusada was ordered to make, in a single night, a Yakushi of a thousand forms, each one to be one foot six inches (Yakushi is the Buddha of healing). And the astrologer Chikamoto was to perform a ceremony 36,000 times in the same amount of time. It is said that in the event, the general recovered in less than one day.

I don't ask you about the 36,000 ceremonies, but how could the thousand images of Yakushi be made in a single night?

TEST

Those in the patriarch's line are said to have the ability to use a thousand hands and a thousand eyes. Use them to make a Yakushi of a thousand forms in an instant. Bring proof of it and show me!

This was first given as a koan to the Buddhist image-maker Yasunori by Zen master Daien (the 3rd teacher at Engakuji).

Imai's note: This story of the Buddhist image-maker Yasusada and how at the official order he made the Yakushi of a thousand forms in a single night appears in a number of writings. There is a matter-of-fact explanation according to which it could be done easily. At that time what was done to make a Yakushi of a thousand forms as a prayer for recovery from illness was to impress a black-ink stamp with the holy picture onto a board and then cut up the latter into sections each with one of them on it. After the ceremony, many of them were thrown into the river. Again there was, and still is, a custom of making seal impressions on to pieces of paper in the same manner. Yasusada would have had a number of apprentices and thus it would have been nothing marvelous for them to turn out a thousand Yakushi representations in one night, perhaps each one making a hundred or so.

But from the point of view of Zen training, as the wording of the test shows, the Zen pupil has to display his skill with a thousand hands and a thousand eyes. If he cannot do that, then however many times he repeats a *dharani* or mantra of the bodhisattva of a thousand hands and eyes, he will not be sure whether it has any effect or not. And then he might as well give up his dazed mumbling and go.

This is something the Zen student has to meditate on. If he becomes one who can use the thousand hands and eyes freely, he will be able to make not merely the Yakushi of a thousand forms, but the three thousand Buddhas of whom they speak at the ordination ceremony, in an instant. If he cannot do it, he may make the Yakushi of a thousand forms, he may pray for recovery from illness, but what will be the use? The one who knows, he alone knows.

NO. 39 *The birth of the Buddha*

Ishida Yamato-no-kami entered upon the Way at Engakuji, where he had Zen interviews with Ikka, who was the 124th teacher there. One day he asked the teacher, "In the scriptures which I have been reading since I began here, there are various different teachings about the day of the Buddha's birth. Which day of which month is the right one?"

The teacher said, "Don't talk about different teachings. When you see the nature to be Buddha, that is the birth of the World-Honoured One."

TESTS

1. If you say, "See the nature to be Buddha," immediately a snake with two heads appears. Are the nature and the Buddha the same or different? If the same, why does it have to tell you to see the nature to be Buddha? If there is a difference, say wherein it is, that seeing the nature is something separate from being Buddha.

2. What is that you recognise when you talk about the nature being Buddha? Say!

This became a Kamakura koan in the interviews of Gyokkei, the 131st teacher at Engakuji.

NO. 46 *Sameness*

In the first year of Shunyu (1241) of the Southern Sung dynasty, priest Rankei (afterward Zen master Daikaku) came to a desire to carry Zen to the east; and in the third month, with five attendants (Gio, Ryosen, Ryuko, Taimon, Kotsugo) he set sail to the east for Hizen (present-day Nagasaki). But when they were passing the coast off Shantung they encountered a typhoon which sank their boat. They managed to transfer to the ship (*Hachiman*) which was making the same voyage, and in the fourth year of Kangen (1247), on the twenty-fourth day of the seventh month, they arrived at Hakata in Kyushu.

(On the first boat) going east to Hizen, when the boat was being driven along by a raging wind and spun around its length by the furious waves, the passengers were terrified, and many had a deathlike aspect. Rankei was saying again and again, "Sameness, sameness" (*Hinten, hinten* – the Japanese approximation to the *p'ing teng* of his Szechuan dialect). "When you put the mind in Sameness with the boat, even if it overturns, that will not trouble you; when you put your mind in Sameness with the waves, even sky-high breakers will not frighten you; when you put your mind in Sameness with life and death, there will be no grieving after the body; when the subject comes to Sameness of mind with the lord, the country is at peace; when the child comes to Sameness with the parents, the family is happy; when the husband comes to Sameness with the wife, their association is perfect; when living beings come to Sameness of mind with the Buddha, delusive passions come to an end. When the Buddha has Sameness of mind with human beings, compassion and virtue appear. To come to the Samadhi of Sameness when approaching or leaving any thing great or small is Bringing-Everything-to-One."

TESTS

1. How do you come to Sameness right now? Say!

2. In the ocean of life and death, the boat of the four great elements (the body) meets a typhoon, and is about

to capsize. At that moment, with what do you come to Sameness? Say!

3. You are sitting in profound meditation when a blazing fire comes toward you and you cannot escape. With what then do you come to Sameness? Say!

4. You are sitting in deep meditation when a ruffian comes to attack you. If you become like him in Sameness of mind, you too will be a ruffian. In such a case how do you understand the real Sameness of mind? Say!

This became a koan in Kamakura Zen in the interviews of Master Kosen.

NO. 48 *The basic truth of Buddhism*

A knight of Ofuna and a student of Zen, Kono Sadakuni, who was avoided by people because of his hasty temper, once came to Master Setsuo, the 25th master at Kenchoji, and shouted at the top of his voice:

"What is the basic truth of Buddhism?"

The teacher told his attendant to light the stove, and said, "Come nearer, come nearer."

The knight again asked, "The basic truth of Buddhism – what is it?"

The teacher beckoned to the attendant to serve him with tea and cakes.

He asked again: "The basic truth of Buddhism – what is it?"

The teacher told the attendant to serve him rice.

Then the knight said, "I thank you indeed for your courteous hospitality. But unfortunately I have still not been told what is the basic truth of Buddhism."

The master said: "The basic truth of Buddhism is nothing more than this: When freezing, to make warm; when parched, to drink; when famished, to eat; when exhausted, to sleep. This is all out in the open before you, with not a speck of anything doubtful. It is the basic truth of spiritual impulse and action, and if the knight has a seeing eye, he will find it under everything I do, walking or standing or sitting or lying down."

The knight thanked him and left. Outside, he said to the attendant: "When I asked the teacher just now about the basic truth of Buddhism, he showed it with fire in the stove, with tea and cakes, and finally with boiled rice. But suppose I met him on the road and asked him about the basic truth of Buddhism, what would he show it with then?"

The attendant said, "Leaving the teacher for a moment, *I* should wave my hands and move my feet to show the basic truth of Buddhism."

The knight said: "Even if I have a seeing eye, suppose you cannot make use of either hand or foot or mouth or nose when I ask what is the basic truth of Buddhism, what will you show it with then?" The attendant was silent.

TEST

Bring a word for the attendant.

This incident became a koan in Kamakura Zen at the interviews of Isei, the 156th master at Kenchoji.

NO. 50 *Reading one's own mind*
A mountain hermit, Jokai of Suwa in Shinano province, made a visit to Zenkoji and had an interview with priest Koho. He

said: "I have been living on Mount Mitake in Shinano for twenty years practicing the arts of the mountain hermits, and now I can easily boil sand and turn it into rice."

The teacher said: "And I have been living here in this temple for twenty years practicing the way of the alchemists of India, and now I can easily take up iron and turn it into gold."

The hermit picked up one of the iron rods that was used as tongs in the stove and handed it to the teacher. Doing this he said, "Let us see you turn this to gold."

The teacher at once took the hermit's hand and pulled it on to the iron pot on the stove, saying: "Instead of my taking the iron and turning it to gold, let us boil you and turn you to rice. Your narrow obstinacy is harder than iron, and if we don't do that first, I won't be able to turn it to gold."

The hermit was impressed and went out, but came back the next day to say, "I have noticed in looking over your Buddhist sutras that there are six supernormal powers in Buddhism (flying, thought-reading, etc.). Can you yourself exercise these powers?"

It happened that a pheasant in the garden gave a cry, and the teacher pointed at it and said: "Even this golden pheasant is exercising them – every time he flies."

The hermit said, "I don't mean that sort of power. Do you for instance have the power to read the minds of others?"

The teacher said, "You should first find out about reading your own mind. If you can't read your own mind, how will you ever read the minds of others?"

The hermit said, "What is this reading one's own mind?"

The teacher said, "An eight-sided grindstone whirling in empty space."

1. What is the method of taking iron and turning it into gold?

2. Is reading one's own mind and reading the mind of others the same thing or different?

This incident became a koan of Kamakura Zen at the interviews of Kohan Shushin of the Obai sub-temple at Engakuji.

NO. 57 *Bukko's death poem*

On the first day of the ninth month of the ninth year of Koan (1286) Bukko, Teacher of the Nation (Kokushi) developed symptoms of illness which he realised he would not survive. He wrote a note to the government officials and old friends to tell them that he would take his departure on the third day of that month.

Just at dawn on the third day he wrote a poem for them:

Buddhas and ordinary men are equally illusions.
If you go looking for the true form, it is a speck of dust in the eye.
The burnt bones of this old monk embrace heaven and earth;
Do not scatter the cold ashes to mountain and sky.

That night at the third watch he changed his robe and, sitting in the meditation posture, took up a brush and wrote:

Coming, and no more going on:
Going, and no more returning.

With a mane of a million hairs, that lion appears:
With its mane of a million hairs, the lion roars.

TESTS

1. Bukko announced the moment of his death three days before. Now, without any promptings, do you declare the time of your own departure? Say!

Imai's note: In this first question, the word "departure" has to be understood in its Zen sense.

2. The Teacher of the Nation said: "Buddhas and ordinary men are equally illusions." Now say: Is there someone who is not illusion, or is there not?

3. Right now who is the one who makes the duality of the illusions? Say!

4. The Teacher said: "The burnt bones of this old monk embrace heaven and earth." Now say: Who is this who embraces the old monk's bones? Speak!

5. The Teacher said: "With its mane of a million hairs, that lion appears, and roars." Now say: Where is this lion roaring right now?

This became a koan at the interviews of Daien, the 3rd master at Engakuji.

NO. 60 *The gravestone with no name*

The gravestone of the priest who founded Hokokuji, by his final instructions, records no name. There is just a great stone on top of the grave to mark the place. Thereafter many of the chief priests of Hokokuji followed this precedent of the founder, and there are many graves without any name on them.

Uesugi Shigemitsu, a student of Zen, once came to Hokokuji and paid his respects to Hakudo, the 5th master there. He said: "At this temple there are gravestones with no name. It will mean that future generations will hardly be able to tell whose graves they are."

The priest said: "After they are dead, what would the line of the priests of this temple want with names? Have you not heard that it is said: 'The four great rivers enter the ocean and lose their name'?"

The nobleman said, "But with the years, the ground may change, and if they do not know the grave, their successors in the dharma will find it impossible to perform the usual worship at the graves of their predecessors."

The master said, "The spiritual gravestones of the line of priests of this temple are in the very depths of the heart of their successors in the dharma. If there is not in Your Honour's own heart the spiritual gravestone of your illustrious ancestor, then worship before even a towering five-storied pagoda will be meaningless."

The noble said, "Your Reverence is the chief priest of this temple of which my illustrious ancestor laid the foundation. Is then the spiritual gravestone of my ancestor in Your Reverence's heart?"

Before he could finish, the priest seized him and threw him down under the pinetree among the graves, and said: "Look, look! Here is the spiritual gravestone, here it is!" The noble grasped a meaning behind the words and said:

"From the very depths of the gravestone without a name come the founder of the temple and the layer of the foundation, holding hands, clear before us!"

1. Hakudo said: "The spiritual gravestones of the line of priests of this temple are in the very depths of the heart of their successors in the dharma." Now say: the line of gravestones in the heart, how do you perform the rite before them, and worship them?

2. How do the founder of the temple and the layer of the foundation hold hands and come before you together? Say!

This incident became a koan in Kamakura Zen at the interviews of Mitsudo, master of Hokokuji.

NO. 65 *How the sutra of The Resolution of the Brahma-king's Doubt was put into the canon*

Atsushige, a warrior who was a student of the Shingon (mantra) sect, came to Jorakuji and asked priest Jikusen about the koans made from scriptures in the so-called *nyorai* Zen, or Buddha Zen. The teacher said: "They are of many kinds. One of them is this: When the Buddha had just been born, he said: 'Above heaven or under heaven, I alone am the world-honoured one.' Then when he completed the path, he declared: 'Wonderful! All beings have innately the nature of the wisdom of the Buddha.'

"Then, before his entry into Nirvana, there was an incident when he held up a flower in his fingers, and there was a smile (from Mahakasypa alone of the spectators). In this case, the meaning of Zen was being presented without any involvement with words at all."

The warrior said: "The incident of the smile comes in the sutra called The Resolution of the Brahma-king's Doubt. But that is not in the canon of authentic scriptures. Probably it was made up by some Zen man of the T'ang dynasty."

The teacher cried: "Atsushige!"

"Yes?" He replied.

"Who has made up this Yes?" said the teacher.

Atsushige made a bow and went out. After three days he had a realization. He came back and said to the teacher: "The sutra of The Resolution of the Brahma-king's Doubt has at last been put in the canon."

TESTS

1. Who was this Brahma-king? Say!

2. How was the Brahma-king's doubt really resolved? Say!

3. What is this putting of the Brahma-king's doubt into the canon?

NO. 73 *Pasting the charm on the heart*

The hall of Yakushi (the Buddha of healing) at Shogonan temple at the pagoda of Hokokuji in Kamakura became widely renowned for its spiritual virtue against plague. After the fighting in the Genko era (1331), there was a succession of epidemics, and Yamanouchi Sadahira asked at the temple for a charm against sickness, adding: "I have heard that the charm must be pasted up on the gate-pillar of one's house. But my own house has been completely burnt during the fighting, and now I have nowhere to live; I am camping under the trees in the valley, and I have no gate-pillar. So how, and where, can I stick this up?"

Daikyo, the priest of Shogonan, said, "Stick it on your heart."

The heart has no form; how can a charm be stuck on to it?

This came to be used as a koan in Kamakura Zen when Daikyo began to give it to test all the Zen students who came to practise *zazen* meditation in the Yakushi hall.

NO. 79 *The lotus strainer*

Yasunaga, a government official and a student of Zen, came to the Dragon Flower of the Golden Peak (the Shinsai-in hall in Jochiji) to pay his respects to priest Musho there. He told him: "These days the followers of Nichiren are saying that in the present degenerate Latter Days, the water of the dharma in the Buddha ocean has become polluted. It is so contaminated that the impurity must be strained off before it is drunk. The only pure water is what has been purified by being strained through the *Lotus Sutra*, and this is the dharma taught by Nichiren. Is what they are saying right?"

The priest said: "Strain off the lotus."

TESTS

1. How would you strain off the lotus?
2. When you have strained and drunk, say how you find it: cold, or hot?

This incident became a koan in Kamakura Zen at the interviews of Toin, the 10th master at Zenkoji.

NO. 94 *Tanka's Buddha-burning*

Imai's note: Tanka was a Chinese Zen master who died in AD 824, and was famous for having burned a wooden Buddha to make a fire on a very cold winter night, there being no other fuel. For this he was severely reprimanded by the superintendent priest of the temple. The latter, however, found his own eyebrows falling off, a traditional sign of something spiritually wrong. There are many pictures of the Buddha-burning incident, including a most unconventional one by Fugai in Japan.

Norimasa, an artist training in Zen, was visiting the Shogatsuan temple of Kamegayatsu (the pagoda of Jufukuji) when he nociced a scroll depicting Tanka burning the Buddha. He asked about the meaning of Tanka's Buddha-burning. Priest Ryozen, who was in charge of the temple, told him: "It is as a means to show how the physical form is destroyed, and with that burning to ashes of the wooden Buddha, the true essence stands out."

The artist said: "I have heard from you the truth of his Buddha-burning. But – I wonder – what did the temple supervisor do wrong that his eyebrows dropped off when he reproved Tanaka so severely?"

The priest said: "Yes, what would he have done wrong? Do you meditate upon it, and penetrate into it."

TESTS

1. Why was it that Tanka burned the Buddha?
2. Why was it that the temple supervisor's eyebrows dropped off?
3. Suppose right now that there is someone in front of

you burning a wooden Buddha, how would you meet the situation?

This incident became a koan in Kamakura Zen at the interviews of Myo-o, the 45th master at Zenkoji and a teacher of the Oryu line.

Part Two

Feudal Zen

THE SPUR IS AN ESSAY FOR SAMURAI, written by Torei, a disciple of Hakuin in eighteenth-century Japan. He wrote this essay in 1755, and it is addressed to a samurai who has faith. So it is in Japanese, and not in Chinese as it might well have been if intended for monks. Torei got it approved by Hakuin, and it was then published.

During the two and a half centuries of peace which Japan enjoyed up to the attack by Western powers in 1854, the samurai had become the administrators of the country. They were not just warriors, though they still had to wear two swords. The Chinese character for the very word "samurai," which is used by Torei, also means "scholar." It is the second element in the compound *haku-shi*, an academic distinction corresponding to a doctorate. Typical is the comment in a classic of 1830 called *Introduction to Budo*, which points out that though the samurai must have a basis of firm, strong character, one who relies on sheer force in his undertakings is bound to make a mess of them. He is like a peasant-farmer pushed into the role of samurai. There has to be learning and culture besides courage and will, it concludes.

The full title of this work is *The Spur for the Good Horse*. A fundamental point in the presentation by Torei is that we already have a good horse. It is not a question of creating one: it is a good horse already. But for some reason, that morning it is feeling a bit dull, or a bit obstinate, or it doesn't grasp what it is supposed to do. And then, just a touch of the spur, and – swish – away it goes. A good horse needs only a touch to recall it to itself. The example is meant as a loose parallel to the Buddha-nature in man. It is so to say a good horse, but somehow it seems to have become dull or darkened or obstinate or destructively minded. So it needs a touch of the spur, and then – swish – it shows itself as it truly is.

A word which Torei uses, normally translated "dye," originally meant something like a smear or grease. But it became confused with another character which looks very similar, and which means the paths of hell. In hell there is a path where you are climbing over sharp swords, and you never come to the end of them, and there is another hell of flames, and so on. So the character can refer to these, but originally it is something like grease, and this sense is characteristic of the text. The mind gets greasy, gets smeared. One teacher commenting on the point gave a kitchen illustration: "You have got to pick up something very hot and move it from here to there. Now if your hand is perfectly clean and dry, and you pick it up and put it down quickly and cleanly, you won't get burned. But if there is any grease or smear on your fingers, any stickiness, then you'll probably get badly burned because you won't be able to just pick it up and let go. There will be a little bit of clinging, and you'll get burned!"

A central point in Torei's exposition is the necessity of purity. It means cleaning off the grease of clinging attachment, or equally clinging hatred, or miry dullness. (Hatred is clinging; we cannot hate people unless we are interested in them.) First of all we must get rid of sticky attachment. It does not mean never taking up things and putting them down: it means not to clutch at them, not to say "I must have that," or "Don't leave me." Because however much we cling, they all simply pass away. While the karma is favourable, they look solid enough and we feel we can hang on to them; but it soon changes, and we suddenly find they were never there at all.

The teaching of the main text is summed up in a few sentences at the beginning: all that is seen, heard, felt, understood, is *hon-shin*. This word means literally heart-essence, explained here with consciousness-only texts. When we see a mountain, we see *hon-shin* in the form of a mountain; when we hear a bird singing, we hear *hon-shin* in the form of bird-song. When we lie down on a straw mat, we lie down on *hon-shin* in the form of a mat.

Then Torei shows how Zen completes the Confucianism, which was the official doctrine for samurai at the time. He points out (as did some Confucians) that it is easy to intone phrases like filial piety, loyalty, and human-heartedness. But most people cannot in fact control their desires and fears, so they fall into evil ways, not stopping at murder of relatives. Zen will enable them to control themselves and follow their principles. If the heart is uncontrolled, then though they look, they do not see, though they listen, they do not hear, and though they eat, they do not taste. One with an uncontrolled heart is like a novice archer who has learned the technique of shooting, but not how to focus on a target. He shoots at random and is entirely destructive. Again he is like a gardener who likes flowers and fruit but does not cultivate the root, because he does not know the connection. The true noble Confucianism can be fully practised when the heart-essence has been attained.

In the same cheerfully eclectic Japanese manner he praises the Way of the Gods (Shinto), Emperor-worship, and the shrine cults in general (though not quite all; some elements of Left Tantrism had crept in). Without realization of the heart-essence, these may drop away into formal rituals.

The traditional history of Zen was important because Zen was being revived in Japan by Hakuin. The Rinzai branch of it had almost died out. All forms of Buddhism had to be authenticated by showing an unbroken transmission from the Buddha-teaching of India, the Holy Land, through the patriarch-transmission of China. Zen teachers were well aware that some of the most revered traditions do not appear in early records. See for instance the koan-story of the Buddha's twirling a flower before the assembly, as set out in No. 65 of the Warrior Koans (see page 61). Nevertheless they maintained the forms and recited them regularly.

He explains at length how warriors have practised Zen at times of crisis, and their example inspired others. If some practise hard, all will go well. In the end, the instruction to a samurai and to a Buddhist nun is the same: practise meditation in rest and in action, till the Buddha-heart stands clear in you. It is urgent repetition of truth, with a view to dispelling illusion by sheer insistence. The method, practised all over the Far East, consists of repeating central truths, with slight variations or even in the original words, again and again. It is effective when the words are repeated verbally with great force, or even when read slowly with strong conviction. The main Buddhist terms are in sonorous Chinese monosyllables; a samurai would have had to read them aloud, slowly, in order to understand them, as there is no redundancy in the written characters. (They correspond to the internationally recognised mathematical symbols, 2, 8, =, %, and so on, which have no one accepted pronunciation, and have to be read carefully.) But reading a translation into an alphabetic script full of redundancies, the eye tends to race over the text, which soon appears merely repetitious and boring. This could be avoided by tape recording the main text with slow enunciation, and then listening to it with concentration.

There are other forms of Kufu; vivid visualization of some of the striking illustrations given in the main text could be one of them.

There is a brief note near the end which echoes one of Hakuin's own writings called *The Koan (riddle) of Illness*: these have been given as directions for when one is ill. But when he is not ill, let him remember not to waste his time either.

IN WHAT ZEN CALLS THE ASCENT from the state of the ordinary vulgar man to the state of Buddha, there are five requirements. First is the principle that they have the same nature. Second is the teaching that they are dyed different colours. Third is the necessity for furious effort. Fourth is the principle of continuity of training. Fifth is the principle of returning to the origin. These five are taught as the main elements of the path.

The true nature with which people are endowed, and the fundamental nature of the Buddhas of the three worlds, are not two. They are equal in their virtue and majesty; the same light and glory are there. The wisdom and wonderful powers are the same. It is like the radiance of the sun illuminating mountains and rivers and the whole wide earth, lighting up the despised manure just as much as gold and jewels. But a blind man may stand pathetically in that very light, without seeing it or knowing anything about it.

Though the fundamental nature of all the Buddhas and of living beings is the same and not distinct, their minds are looking in quite different directions. The Buddha faces inward and makes the heart-essence (*hon-shin*) shine forth. The ordinary man faces outward, and is concerned with the ten thousand things.

For what he likes, he develops strong desire; for what he does not like, he develops hatred; when his thinking becomes rigid, he is stupefied. Bewildered by one of these Three Poisons, he turns into a clutching ghost, or a fighting demon ablaze with fury, or an animal. When they are equally mixed in him, he falls into hell, where he suffers in so many ways. These are called the Four Evil States, and they are dreadful. If despite his greed and anger and dullness, he does control himself at least to some extent, he becomes human. Life after life he holds on in the human form. Then, although still not having cut off greed and anger and delusion altogether, the self-control being incomplete, he is born – selfish as he still is – in some paradise. There are six of these so-called Heavens of Desire. Then when the fundamental nature of the Three Poisons has been annihilated, meditation and wisdom manifest in him; but his meditation is on Love, and residual traces of anger and apathy remain. So he is born somewhere in the Eighteen Worlds-with-form. Even when the meditation on Love reaches its limit, the knowledge-vision of the Buddha has not yet opened in him. He is now born in one of the Four Worlds-without-form, where dwell the Truth-Hearers and the Buddhas-for-themselves-alone. All the states first described – the four bad ones, the human, and the heavenly ones – when taken together comprise the Six Paths of the World-Process. If we now add to them the Truth-Hearers, Buddhas-for-themselves-alone, bodhisattvas, and the Buddhas, it comes to a total of ten.

Generally speaking, out of the Six Paths, pleasures might seem to be experienced in the human world or in a heavenly one, but in fact it is all pain. How is this? It is because these worlds are based on hearts deeply sunk in agonies of greed, anger, and dullness, and experienced by them as such. So if passions are not lessened, there is no escape from the Six

Worlds of Suffering. If they are not escaped, there can never be real peace and happiness.

If one wants to get out of the worlds of suffering, first of all one has to realise how they are all the time passing away. What is born, inevitably dies. Youth cannot be depended on, power is precarious, wealth and honour crumble away. High status requires constant vigilance to preserve it. The longest life hardly gets beyond eighty years. Since therefore it is all melting away, there is nothing enjoyable about it. The badly off suffer from not having things; the well-off suffer from having them. The high suffer from being highly placed, and the despised suffer from being lowly placed. There is suffering connected with clothes and food, suffering with the family, suffering from wealth and possessions, suffering from official rank.

So long as the nature is not freed from passions, and the path of seeking release has not been found, then even supposing there were some king and his ministers, glorious like a god among living sages, it would all be insubstantial like a lightning flash or a dewdrop under the morning sun – gone in a moment.

When karma happens to be favourable, these things appear solid enough, but as the favourable karma dissipates, it turns out that there was never anything there at all. By favour of the karma of our parents we have got this body, and by favour of the earth, the skin and flesh and sinew and bone grow. By favour of water, the blood and body fluids come, and by favour of fire, warmth, harmony, softness, and order come to be. By favour of winds, vitality, breath, movement, and change come about. If these four favourable karmas suddenly become exhausted, then breathing ceases, the body is cold, and there is nothing to be called "I." At that time this body is no true "I." It was only ever a rented accommodation.

However clingingly attached to this temporary abode, one cannot expect it to last forever. To realise the Four Noble Truths, that all this is passing, painful, empty, and without a self, and to seek the way of *bodhi*-intelligence, is what we call the Dharma of Hearing the Noble Truths.

If you would grasp the nature of the universal body of all the Buddhas, first you must be clear about, and then you must enlighten, the root of ignorance in you. How is it to be made clear? You must search after your true nature. How to search? In the eye, seeing of colours; in the ear, hearing of sounds; in the body, feeling distinctions of heat and cold; in the consciousness, feelings of wrong and right: all these must be seen clearly as they are. This seeing and hearing and knowing is at the root of the practice. The ordinary man sees colours and is deluded by colours, hears voices and is deluded by voices, feels heat and cold and is deluded by heat and cold, knows right and wrong and is deluded by right and wrong. This is what is meant by the saying: "The ordinary man looks outward."

The training of a bodhisattva is: when looking at some colour, to ask himself what it is that is being seen; when hearing some sound, to ask himself what it is that is being heard; when feeling hot or cold, to ask himself what it is that is being felt; when distinguishing wrong from right, to ask himself what it is that is being known. This is called the "facing inward of the Buddhas." Practicing it is different from facing in the direction in which the ordinary man looks. At first, though facing the same way as the Buddha, the Buddha power and wisdom are not manifest in him. But still, he is a baby bodhisattva, and he must realise that he has come into that company. If he always keeps to his great vow to the Buddhas, praying to the spiritual lights and being loyal to the teacher, then one day the Great Thing comes about, and he is set free in the ocean of Own-good is Others' good.

When you get up in the morning, however much business there may be waiting, first affirm this one thought, first turn to this meditation on seeing and hearing. After that, engage in the activities of the day. When going to have a meal or a drink, first of all you must try to bring this one thought to the fore, and make a meditation on it. When you go to wash your hands, first you should try to bring this thought uppermost in your mind and meditate on it. When last thing at night you are going to lie down, sit for a little bit on the bedclothes and try to bring this thought to the fore and meditate; then lie down to sleep. This is practicing the true path of Buddhas and bodhisattvas. Whip up your enthusiasm for it by realizing how if you fail to grasp your true nature as one with the nature of Buddha, you will be lost in the wheel of continual rebirth, circling endlessly in the Four Births and Six Worlds.

From the beginning, you must learn to put your whole heart into this basic meditation, going ahead with each thought and practicing on each occasion as it comes up. Keep up the right line of the meditation: when you walk, practise while walking; when you sit still, practise while sitting; when talking to people, practise while talking. When there is no talking and things are quiet, then you can meditate more intensely. When you look at things, ask yourself what it is that you see; when you hear things, ask yourself what it is that you hear. When things get very rushed so that you easily get swept away by them, ask yourself what this is, that you should get swept away by it. And even if you do get swept away, don't give up your meditation. If you get ill, use the pain as the seed-subject for your meditation.

In every circumstance, the meditation must go forward in a straight line, however much business there may be. It is not allowable that the meditation should be vivid and clear only when the surroundings are familiar and quiet. Unless the meditation is bright and clear at all times, it cannot be said to have power. If there is an outbreak of armed strife in a country which has to be stopped, at the critical time it is a question of taking the field, confronting the dangers, and fighting fearlessly without ever thinking of turning back – that is the way to victory. The meditation-fight is the same. It is just when you are caught up in situations where your thoughts are disturbed, that there is a chance to win a decisive victory.

Be aware of this heart of yours. See that it does not weaken, and go forward. In fact when things are quiet, it corresponds to the time when warriors are safe within the castle, when they must train themselves in tactics and strategy. They practise with courage and sincerity. When the country is disturbed by armed uprisings, they know that this is the time to go out to the field of battle and decide the issue. You must meditate with just such a strong resolve. You may not have the power of the Buddhas yet, but you are one of those who are on the Way of all the Buddhas.

It is a fact that little enlightenment obstructs great enlightenment. If you give up any little enlightenment you may have, and do not clutch it to yourself, then you are sure to get great enlightenment. If you stick at the little enlightenment and will not give it up, you are sure to miss the great enlightenment. It is like someone who sticks to little profits, and so misses the big ones. But if he does not hang on to little profits, he will surely be able to get big ones. When the little profits are not clung to, but invested bit by bit, it does end in a big profit. Similarly, if you stick to the little profit of little enlightenment, so that the whole life is a succession of experiences of little enlightenments, you will never be able to reach the great freedom, the great release. If you don't find the way to the great freedom through great enlightenment, your individual applications (*ji*) will not accord with the great principle (*ri*), and you will fall into the wrong views of outsiders-away-from-Buddhism. It is terrible. But if, when you have a little enlightenment, you take that as a seed and go forward steadily, further and further with your practice, then the great profit of all the Buddhas becomes fully manifest. You will naturally pass through the barrier-riddles (*kansho*) set by the patriarchs. Now indeed, individual application and universal principle are in accord, action and understanding are not separate. You attain the state of great release, the great freedom. It is for this that stress is laid on maintaining the practice.

Now when you have penetrated into the truth wholly, all the powers of the Way are brought to fulfilment, all beings everywhere are blessed whenever any opening presents itself. Though you may indeed preach and teach, really there is nothing lacking: "I" and the others all attain the shore of the fourfold Nirvana.

Through the great operation of the great vow, beings and worlds benefit themselves as well as others, and you must resolve never to turn away from it in the future. In the present meantime, there may be mistakes and lapses; legs are weak and the path slippery. If you don't get up when you've fallen down, surely you'll be destroyed. You will die where you've fallen. But if, though falling, you pull yourself up, and falling again, pull yourself up again, and so go ahead further and further, finally you do reach the goal. The sutra says: "If you have broken a commandment, make your repentance before the Buddha at once: then go forward along the Way."

Intensifying the meditation practice in the way described, when the practice becomes clear and mature, you finally return to his nature, one with that of all the Buddhas. This is what they call Becoming Buddha. When it is said in Zen, See the Nature to Be Buddha, this is what is meant. At the beginning, owing to the one delusion, the True Nature (*Hon-shin*) which should face inward, is made to circle outwardly in the Six Paths: of hell, clutching ghosts, animals, demons, men, and heavens, rising and sinking like the rim of a chariot wheel through thousands of lives in millions of world-cycles, interminably. The bones of birth after birth would pile up higher than mountain peaks, and the life-blood would overflow the great ocean. So teaches the Buddha. Now having achieved human birth, hard to attain, and having come across his holy doctrine, rarely to be found, and of that doctrine to be able to hear the wonderful truth called the *Mahayana*, such is to be reckoned the most fortunate of beings. If you fail to take it up or openly reject it, that must be reckoned the greatest of sins. Once lost, it is as difficult to regain the human birth as it would be for a thread lowered from the highest heaven to enter the eye of a needle on the bottom of the ocean.

And the circling in the Six Paths is not just a question of reincarnation. In one single day here people are rising and sinking in it. When the heart is right and avoids wrong, that is a man. When others oppose him and hatred for them arises, that is a furious demon. When one has sticking attachment for what one likes, he becomes a clutching ghost. When the heart gets stuck in thinking of material things, he is an animal. If, even though he does think deeply, attachment is strong, if the flames of anger do not cease, and he seeks to injure others, then he is in hell. All this is losing the path of humanity and sowing seeds of the Three Poisons. Then again there may be a time when the heart is peaceful, not thinking about material things, and there is inner purity; now, though in a human body, his heart is truly said to be sporting in heaven. But in general, people do not realise how they are circling in the Six Paths in a single day. In fact those who attain to human-heartedness are few, what to say of sporting in heaven? Most are sporting in the Three Poisons of animal materialism, ghost hankering, and demon hatred. If they change at all, it is mostly to fall into the paths of hell, tormenting others and destroying everything. See the paths in which we are reincarnating in the course of just one day!

At first, the heart is on the wrong paths two-thirds of the time, with the human being barely holding on to one third. Then again hell comes up in it. So it is that living an ordinary life, it is difficult to get away from those wrong paths. But if in the course of the day there arises some resolve at practice, of the Four Principles of the Truth-Hearers, or the doctrine of Twelve Links of Dependence of the Lone Buddhas, or the Six Perfections of the Bodhisattva Way, then in that heart, seeds of the Three Poisons will be destroyed. He who strives to intensify his practice, finally attains realization; even before he does so, since the poisons in the heart have ceased, he will pass beyond temporary joys of human and heavenly worlds, and ascend to the higher state. Truth-hearers and Solitaries are already noble, what to say of one on the path of the bodhisattva? That path is already so difficult to attain, what to say of the dharma of the Buddha Way? The Zen realization of Seeing the Nature is the very crown of all Buddhahood. He who has his heart set on this is already a baby Buddha. Thought after thought, he steps out toward the gate of peerless merit, along the way of holy perfection. Wonderful is the merit even of reading about such perfection, what to say of practicing it? Even to get another to read it aloud will save one from disaster of fire, so what shall we say of one who practises it himself? The Buddhas bless him, the bodhisattvas stretch out their hands to him, the gods in their heavens applaud him. At a glimpse of his shadow, demons and evil spirits are routed. Spirits imprisoned in the depths, by contact with him realise the opportunity of release. This is called the highest, noblest, and very first dharma. Step by step it must be faithfully followed out.

Part Three

Modern Zen

TSUJI SOMEI IS A PRESENT-DAY ROSHI who trained under Furukawa Gyodo, one of the great figures in Zen of the first half of the twentieth century, who taught at Engakuji, in Kamakura, thirty miles from Tokyo. These extracts are translated from his autobiography, and have been selected (with Tsuji Roshi's permission) to focus on the Zen training.

Mr. Tsuji married early and got a job as an accountant with a big oil company. He became interested in possible political solutions to social problems. His wife contracted tuberculosis and died early, leaving him with the children to look after. He later married again.

Treading the Way of Zen
The Autobiography of Tsuji Somei

MY FIRST VISIT TO A MONASTERY TO PRACTISE ZEN was in the summer of 1925, when I was twenty-two and in my first year at the Tokyo University of Commerce [now the prestigious Hitotsubashi University—Tr.] I was one of a student group at the university who practised Zen meditation, and every year our group joined similar ones from other universities to go to Engakuji in Kamakura for a week's intensive instruction and training.

Furukawa Gyodo Roshi was then the abbot of the monastery, and at my first interview with him, he asked:

"Why have you come here?"

I replied: "Because I can't sleep well."

He commented: "That's because you bother yourself over idle thoughts even when you're in bed," and laughed.

I still recall this little scene vividly.

Sitting in the meditation posture for hours and hours, day and night, proved a hard task indeed: the pain in my legs was almost unbearable. Still, after the practice ended, I could sleep unusually well, and when I woke up the next day I thought to myself: "Last night I slept like a log." In itself this was trivial, but the pleasure of this first sound sleep in many nights increased the pull to Zen.

During that first week I was impressed at the sight of the young monks working. To see them sweeping the extensive grounds with bamboo-twig brooms, in perfect silence and with full attention, put me in mind of the intensity of fencers practicing, and I felt a sort of reverence for them. It was also striking to see them walking rapidly, with their hands clasped over the breast and looking straight ahead.

In the early morning we followed them in ladling a little cold water with a dipper, from the large common basin into the hollow of one hand, to wash the face. Again, when the slippers were taken off before entering the meditation hall, they had to be set down perfectly aligned, with the toes pointing outward so that the owner could smoothly slip the feet into them when leaving.

While keeping up my studies of social problems, I did not drop my interest in religion. Sometimes I went to Kamakura to have an interview with Master Gyodo, and I also attended lectures by other Zen masters in Tokyo itself. In those days I could make nothing of them, or even of those by Master Gyodo, and had a private impression of the croaking of frogs. But I was deeply impressed by his character and, when something important came up, I often went to him for advice.

I remember that once I was puzzling over the inconsistency between my profession as an accountant in a commercial firm and my religious aspirations; I had nearly decided to enter some other career. I went to the Roshi and told him what I was proposing to do. He listened in silence to all that I had to say, and then curtly remarked: "This is just your vanity." It was like a great blow with a staff, crushing my deeply considered decision. Afterward I gradually came to realise that he was right.

One day I found myself in the guest room for an interview with the Roshi along with one other visitor, an elderly man.

There was no difference at all in the Master's attitude to him, and to the obscure young man that I was. Later on I asked who the old man had been, and discovered that he was a millionaire named Machida, who used to invite Master Gyodo to take monthly Zen sessions at his mansion. I was deeply impressed by the perfect equality with which the Roshi had treated the two of us.

For a hundred days after my wife's death I chanted sutras, and repeated the invocation for a considerable time morning and evening. My three little children often kept company with me during these practices. Often at night I lay in bed with my arms stretched out to each side so that my children could hold my hands while falling asleep.

Meanwhile, I had begun to realise that one might engage in reform movements, political, economic, or social, but if one had not transcended his ego, one would be found to be acting for fame or power in the end, though claiming to be devoted to nation or society. I saw that it was a matter of paramount importance in life for any man to investigate what was his own true nature, and to get completely rid of his petty ego.

About that time I met one of my former classmates at the university, who had been practicing Zen under the guidance of Abbot Ashikaga Shogan. A lay disciple's name, Hakutei, had been conferred on him by his teacher after he had the experience of "seeing the true nature." He remarked to me: "Before I had seen into the true nature of my being, I used to practise meditation like mad." Stirred by these words, I began to practise meditation not only at home but also in the electric train on my way to work. At the office I would avail myself of any spare time to sit and meditate behind a screen of account books. At the lunch break, I went into the reception room for the same purpose.

From the first of November that year, there was an intensive meditation week at Engakuji. I went to it with do-or-die resolution to see my inmost nature at any cost, though I had only been able to get three days leave from the company. I was then thirty-five years old. For the first three days I sat with the monks in the meditation hall. My mind was wholly absorbed in the endeavour to keep in the right frame of mind all the time. Once at a meal I forgot to pick up the chopsticks, and another time during the single-file walking (*kinhin*) which is part of the meditation, I was so abstracted that I stumbled and fell. The meditations began at three in the morning, and ended at ten at night, but when the day's sitting had come to an end, I felt as if all the hours had passed in a moment. As I look back to my experiences at the time, I find I was in the state technically called "infinite darkness."

At the end of my three days, I had still not attained to seeing the inmost nature. Filled with disappointment, I left the temple. In the electric train on the way back, however, I suddenly experienced an extraordinary inner change. I saw light issuing from the forehead of all my fellow passengers; as I looked, I saw light coming from every object.

After a walk of a quarter of a mile from the station, I got back, and felt an ecstasy welling up within me. I was dancing about the room, literally not knowing how my arms moved, or where my steps trod, as the saying is. Overwhelmed by the strangeness of what was happening, I went back at once to Engakuji and asked for special permission to see the Master. This was not granted, however, because it was so late, so I went to the lay disciples' quarters and sat up meditating the rest of the night. The next morning when I related my experience to the Master, he replied: "While you feel ecstatic, you have not yet gotten there." Then he recited in a low voice a passage from the *Record of Rinzai*: "The mind adapts itself to all situations, and its manner of adaptation is most subtle. If you realise your nature in the very process of flowing, you will neither rejoice nor grieve." Then he added: "If you can understand this saying, you will have seen into your nature."

When I arrived at the company the next day, the head of my section greeted me jocularly with the remark: "Well, Mr. Tsuji, you certainly seem to have had some good news from somewhere, to have such a shining forehead."

From this time I kept up the meditation with the utmost intensity. Almost every day I went to Kamakura, passing the nights alternately at home and at Engakuji.

One day after our interview, my teacher Gyodo Roshi said to me: "You come here so often to see me. But are your children well cared for? Even the best medicine should be taken in moderation."

I replied, "But Master, shouldn't iron be struck while it's hot?"

At this, the Roshi looked as though he had swallowed something down, but did not say a word.

Now the newspapers were piling up on my big desk sometimes for weeks together, unread. Though I was in the business world, I begrudged the time for reading them and devoted it to meditation instead. My income did not allow for much margin, and on the trips to Engakuji I used to take some packets of food with me to eat on the way, with a bottle of plain water in the bag as well. As it was now late autumn and then winter, the meal was always cold. Still, I was finding it very tasty and the thought came to me how, when the mind is completely one-pointed, even plain boiled rice and cold water become delicious.

There is a Zen saying: "The heart magnanimous, like an emperor," and I found that my inner state was of itself becoming somehow wide and full, and the greatness of the Zen path was borne in on me more and more. I resolved that I would do everything I could to preserve this great traditional path of the East.

About this time I was reading almost no Zen books except the *Record of Rinzai*, and Master Hakuin's *Tea-kettle* classic. In this latter I came across a verse quoted from the great Chinese layman of the Tang dynasty called Master Fu:

Empty-handed, holding a plough:
Walking, riding a water buffalo:
When the man crosses the bridge,
The bridge flows and the water does not.

Hakuin said that if one could see right through into this verse, he would see his own true nature.

One morning in November that year, when on the way from Engakuji to work at my company I was walking on the platform of Tokyo station, suddenly the realization of

"Walking, riding a water-buffalo" came to me. It was like a flash: "This is it!" While writing at the office, the realization of "Empty-handed, holding a plough" came too. Then in the bus on the way home, I penetrated the last phrases of Master Fu's verse. This was a case of coming to the realization of a Zen koan before having it set formally by the master.

Still, it was some time before my master would sanction my attempts at the koan which he had actually set me. In his interview room (which was called the Poisonous Wolf Cave), he used to urge me to go deeper into it, saying: "Now is the time when you must store up the energy to last you through your entire spiritual career." Looking back, I am grateful indeed for the unyielding firmness of the Master's training.

One day toward the end of November, I was in the interview room presenting my understanding of the koan: "Why is it called Mount Sumeru?" As the teacher spoke, a cry burst from me with the realization throughout my whole being that my true nature was no nature, that the limited and relative self is in fact unlimited and absolute. It was a realization of infinite self in direct experience. It was knowing nothingness to the limit of negation. At that moment of that day, in the Poisonous Wolf Cave, I felt I had been reborn.

From that time onward, when koans were set, I often found solutions to them bubbling up spontaneously within me, to pass me through.

In January of the next year, the teacher gave me the lay name So-mei (The Bright One), and the full Buddhist name Daiki-in So-an So-mei (The Dark-bright Pair in the Hall of Great Power). I later discovered that these two names refer to the Dark-bright Pair in the verse by I'Ts'un at the end of Case 51 of *The Blue Cliff Record*.

One morning I was going up the slope in the grounds of Engakuji to have an interview with Master Gyodo. It was about dawn. I happened to meet him by the little lake called Myoko (Delicate Scent), which is just below the rise on which the Master's interview room stood.

"Where are you going?" he asked.

"I was hoping to have an interview about my koan," I replied.

"Then I'll hear your answer here," he told me.

So standing on my side of the lake in the faint light, I submitted my solution.

After the interview, he said: "Let us walk together."

Walking behind him, I followed him down the gradual slope toward the temple gate. As soon as we reached the road in front of the temple, he returned by another way.

This was before the time for the regular interviews for the monks living in the monastery, and so early that as yet none of the rays of the sun streaked the sky. The Master wore a pair of wooden clogs, on high supports, and went briskly and calmly along the rugged stony road despite the dark. Seeing him going so fast in the awkward footgear, along a road where even a young man in broad daylight would have to walk with care, I had an inkling of the spiritual energy that had come to my teacher through Zen. He was then about sixty-four.

In December 1936, the year when I had "seen the nature" (*kensho*), I moved from my home in Ogikubo in the suburbs of Tokyo to a place in the street in front of Engakuji. This was so that I could have more opportunities for evening interviews with Master Furukawa, even though living in Tokyo, I had been able to get to the temple for the regular interviews in the morning. They began at four a.m. in June and July, but when it came to December and January they would be held a little after six o'clock. So it was not impossible for me to get down to Kamakura, have an interview, and then be back for work in Tokyo. I used to get up quietly and steal out so as not to disturb the family, and could arrive in Kamakura, climb the dark road up the hill, and be on time.

The evening interviews were a little past seven p.m. in June and July, but in the winter months they began just after five o'clock, and as my office duties came to an end at that time I could not possibly manage the interviews during this part of the year. This was a matter of great regret to me.

At Engakuji there were also week-long special intensive meditation periods (*sesshin*) held four times during the winter months, and four times during the summer. I tried to attend these as often as I could, but my office duties interfered. Also, there was always the possibility that I could be transferred by the company to a branch office in Osaka or Shimonoseki at any time.

I was now devoted to Zen as a noble ideal and resolved to follow it right through. I also wanted to change my present profession for some other which would afford more time and opportunities for Zen. It happened that at the end of 1937, Professor Masao Hisataka (then at Yokohama College and later at Hitotsubashi University), who was a friend of mine, visited our office to inquire about the prospects of employment there next year for some of the promising students of his college. I took the opportunity of talking to him about my own enthusiasm for Zen and my desire for a change of profession which would give me more scope to pursue it.

Early in March the next year, he sent me a card saying that the principal of his college would like to see me, if I would kindly visit him. When I met him he offered me a professorship – I was to teach accounting and bookkeeping.

Apart from my professional qualification, this was what I had been doing at the Kokura Oil Company for the past nine years, during which time I had been promoted from a clerk to a deputy secretary, now receiving a sizeable income plus the regular half-yearly bonuses. But as the new position would provide only perhaps a third of what I had been getting, I put the matter to my wife and explained the circumstances to her. We agreed that we should have to change our style of living completely. As far as spiritual life was concerned, however, I could enjoy a much more congenial and enriched life. Apart from the joy of being able to participate in the morning and evening interviews every day now as well as in the special meditation periods much more regularly, I found teaching more congenial. It was a pleasure to do the preparatory work for the lecture and to teach and talk to students. We often had friendly talks in small restaurants near the college, and some of them used to come to see me at home.

On the surface, teaching is much easier than office work, but in fact I began to feel that I was carrying a heavy burden on my back all the time. It turned out that actually I had less time free from duties than when I had been working in an office. Only during the vacations did I have plenty of free time to spend just as I liked. It is indeed the holidays that are the great advantage of the teaching profession.

One summer vacation I passed about forty days almost entirely away from home. I lodged in the Lay-Disciples' Hall in Engakuji, and often sat in meditation in the Founder's Shrine at the Obai-in sub-temple, which is in the Engakuji complex. I gave up shaving, and grew a long beard. One night I decided to sit up all night in meditation in the Lay-Disciples' Hall. As time went on, I became overwhelmed by drowsiness, and finally I lay down where I was, resting my head on one arm. I was suddenly awakened by something dropping on my forehead. To my drowsy perceptions, it seemed to be something quite big. Once fully awake, I realised that it was a large centipede creeping over my neck. I swept it away with my hand. There are many such things in the temple precincts.

At this time of my life, I often slept only three or four hours a night. I suppose that even a few hours will suffice if the sleep becomes deep as the result of the coming-to-one of the mind through the practice of Zen meditation.

In the Hakuin tradition, the occasion when the master grants interviews to a disciple, which take place in his living quarters, is called *shitsu-nai* (inside the room). At the interview, the disciple confronts his master man-to-man, presenting his answer to the koan riddle for the master's judgment and engaging in question-and-answer with him. The interview is also termed *hossen*, or spiritual warfare. It is the most important and solemn occasion in Zen training. Masters' particular ways of training and their spiritual attainments are manifested through their words and actions "inside the room."

There was a calmness, as of the depths of the ocean, about Master Gyodo "inside the room," and also something of what in Zen is called the sheerness of a silver cliff or an iron wall. He hardly ever resorted to slapping or yelling. But sometimes when he rejected my answer to a koan with the words, "That won't do," I felt as if I had indeed been slapped in the face, or thundered at with the usual Katzu! shout.

In the interview room with Master Gyodo it was quiet, but there was a feeling of severity and something terrifying.

One winter I caught cold, and a rheumatic knee condition which I had from childhood flared up, so that I could not bend my left knee at all. If I had to squat down, I stuck out my left leg straight in front, and went down on the bent right knee. I had to use a stick when going from home to the interviews at the temple. But when I came before the teacher to make my prostration, the knee could suddenly bend. It was quite extraordinary. When I left to make my way back home, on the other hand, the knee again could not bend.

Another thing that happened to me was a persistent fit of hiccups, which lasted about a week. There was a popular idea that to go on hiccuping for more than a certain number of days would result in death, and I did all the things that are supposed to cure hiccups, but all was in vain. Yet during the interview with the Master, and for some time afterward, the hiccups used to cease. And then they would come back again. This seems perhaps a small matter, but I can never forget it.

At an interview, the Master and I would sit on the ground, face to face, with only perhaps five or six inches between our knees. Although we were so close, sometimes he spoke in such a low voice I could not make out what he was saying. But when I would be walking quietly back along the corridor to the room where the other monks were waiting to strike the bell in their turn to have an interview, his voice seemed as it were to get stronger and stronger in me so that I could easily understand what had been said to me. This too is one of my special memories of the interviews in the Poisonous Wolf Cave.

I was in the special category of what is called *tsuzan*, so that I could often ask for *naizan*, which means an interview outside the normal fixed times. To someone in a situation like myself, Master Gyodo would cheerfully give interviews.

At the end of the year in which I had "seen the nature," I asked for one of these interviews, though it was New Year's Eve. Although the next day was the great festival day of New Year, I turned up as usual in the evening and asked for the interview. But the Master's attendant refused me, just saying: "New Year..." Only then did I think: "Why, yes, it's New Year"; but then the thought came too: "Did not the ancients warn us that change is upon us: time does not wait on man"?

Perhaps I was at that time really steeped in Zen, as the saying goes.

There are some other things I shall always remember about him. Once he caught a cold which led to a high fever. His throat was painful, and his voice terribly hoarse. We were very worried, but he wrapped several lengths of cloth around his throat, and gave the sermons at the *sesshin* in a sort of strangled voice. After the session was over, I presented myself to pay my respects and asked after him; he just said: "Oh, today I brushed some Chinese calligraphy, so it's all right again."

When he was in good health, his voice was vibrant and very clear. In fact when I first took to going to hear him, it was not so much the content of the address as the attraction of his voice that drew me. At the public ceremonies, he would pass in front of us listeners to make the three bows before the Buddha, and his posture as he passed, and his tread as he went up to the shrine to light a stick of incense, had for me a sort of indescribable magic about them.

Usually he used to walk around the temple complex before dawn each morning, but apart from that, he did not leave his private quarters much, so that even in the grounds he was not often to be met. I was once standing in front of the laymen's hall when he came out from his own quarters walking toward the temple gate. I bowed my head and the Roshi brought his palms together in the traditional salutation, pursuing his way without the slightest check. I had the feeling of the Zen saying: "Walk like the wind." At that time he was, I suppose, about sixty-seven or sixty-eight.

Another typical incident was this: I was to see him about something, and presented myself at the back door of his quarters, before the sliding door of his attendant's room. I announced myself, and heard the Roshi's own voice: "What do you want?" When I slid open the door, I saw him bent right down, having his head shaved by the attendant monk. In that very awkward position, and accosted unexpectedly, his voice still seemed to come from the depths of his being, and I got an idea of what must have been the thousand temperings and polishings of his training over the long years.

Here are a few things from those days with Master Gyodo which still often come to my mind:

• Zen is something about which someone who doesn't really know can still manage to write without giving himself away. But if you hear him speak just a couple of words, you know his inner state exactly.

 • For Seeing the Nature, it has to be fierce as a lion, but after that realization, the practice has to go slow like an elephant.

• If you get through the first barrier (the first koan) without much trouble, you get stuck afterward and can't get on. It's as if you'd thrust your hand into a glue pot.

• However much you go to Zen interviews, and however many koans you notch up, if you don't get to the great peace...

• Going simply by the number of koans you pass – well, however many they may be, it's no good unless you come to the *samadhi* of no-thought. In the *samadhi* of no-thought, there's no soul, there's no body, there are no objects of the senses, much less any koan!

• For Going the Rounds (visiting a number of teachers in turn for interviews) you have got to have an eye that can see a teacher.

• You have to be able to enter freely and come out of the world of the absolute (infinite non-distinction) or the world of the relative (limited distinction) at will.

• You may go the rounds, but unless you learn the strong points of each teacher, you will get nothing out of it. If you are simply looking for weak points in teachers, however much you may go round it will be no good.

• I can't understand what they call reputation in the world. There are people who, when you go and see them, are completely different from what you have heard about them.

• Whatever koan it may be, it comes down to the absolute, or the relative, or an unobstructed harmony of absolute and relative.

• When one has attained realization (*satori*) the practice has to be taken to the point where even the first syllable, *sa*, meaning "distinguishing," has ceased to exist.

• (Of a certain teacher.) He is supposed to be a teacher, but I find something peculiar about him; and somehow even what he writes has got a smell about it.

• If someone goes right through the training, he goes back to his original temperament. With one who likes rice-wine, it's rice-wine; with one who likes women, it's women – that's the sort of thing.

Note by Tsuji Roshi: This remark by Master Gyodo did not mean assenting to sexual practices and other desires: the one who has gone right through the training has come to the state of the true no-I (*mu-ga*) and no-Minding (*mu-shin*). The Master is pointing here to the heart of heavenly truth, the great life of nature. I feel that this was what was meant by Confucius when he said: "At seventy years of age, I could follow the desires of my heart, and they never transgressed the moral rules."

• A man who does things without "hidden virtue" (*on-doku*) will surely have no good end to his life.
• So-and-so Roshi used to say he wanted to test teachers, and went round to a number of training halls, boasting of "taking away their announcement bells" and so on. But this sort of thing has no hidden virtue about it, and so his last years were not good.
• In Case 19 of the *Mumonkan* collection of koans, called "The Ordinary is the Way," Mumon has a comment: "Even when Joshu had realised, he had to start on a further thirty years of practice." I asked about this thirty years, and Master Gyodo said: "Thirty years means the lifetime, practice is the whole life long."

In his sermons, when the subject of the Sixth Patriarch Eno came up, Master Gyodo seemed to burn with enthusiasm as he spoke of how the patriarch had a first enlightenment on hearing a phrase from the *Diamond Sutra*, that the mind should move without making a home anywhere, had gone to Mount Obai to be under Master Konin, and there was treated not as a priest but as a lay pilgrim and set to pounding rice, and how he was recognised through the poem: "The *Bodhi* (wisdom) is not a tree, nor has the mirror any stand: from the very beginning not a single thing – on what could the dust alight?" Then how he was chosen as successor out of the hundreds of disciples, and entrusted with the Transmission by the Fifth Patriarch, who helped him to leave Obai secretly under cover of darkness to escape the jealousy and spite of some other disciples.

• There is a Zen phrase: "In the cold, the hair stands on end." When the Master used to speak of these dramatic events in the history of Chinese Zen, I experienced this literally. The impact of his words was so tremendous that I felt my hair standing on end.

• Around about this time my favourite reading was the lives of Shido Bunan and Shoju Rojin, teacher of Hakuin. Occasionally Master Gyodo used to say something to the effect that perhaps things were going to become something like they were in the times of Bunan and Shoju. He said that though they were priests, in fact they had much of the attitude of laymen (*koji*), and that possibly in the future, for a time, the dharma might be propagated by these laymen.

🔱

Around then I also came to study enthusiastically the lives of the historic National Teachers Daito and Muso, and I went all the way to Shogenji at Ibuka in Mino province where Muso used to live, and to the Kazan temple in Kyoto, to pay reverence to the tomb of Gudo, who had been a teacher of Shido Bunan.

In 1940 Master Gyodo retired from being head of the Engakuji sect, and went back to the Tenchian hermitage at Kuboyama in the district of Yokohama. At that time his room was at the back of the temple, and on his desk was a goldfish bowl, which someone had brought him. It was set on a light stand made of bamboo cross-pieces. One day, after the Zen interview, I was talking to the teacher when a bee flew into the room, seemed to dance around happily, and then went into the hollow of one of the bamboo pieces of the goldfish bowl stand. Another time when I was there just the same thing happened: I saw a bee fly in and go into the bamboo tube. I got the impression that the Master – so strict and forbidding to pupils – was to this bee a kindly playmate. In this side of the Roshi's character I saw an affinity with Master Ikkyu (some four hundred years before), who had a pet sparrow which he called his attendant. When the sparrow died, he gave him a posthumous Buddhist name, Sonrin, and wrote a death poem for him.

The Master had once told me himself how, when he was still in charge of Jochiji, in his forties, he had been lying asleep with almost nothing on and a large venomous centipede had crawled across his chest. He had not brushed it off and killed it but let it go on its way. When I saw how the bee seemed to be playing in the Master's room, I recalled that story about the centipede.

It is fair to say that up to the time of my call-up into the army in June 1941, I spent almost all the spare time allowed by my professional work in Zen interviews and study. There were times of tension and times of relaxation, but throughout I was treading the path of Zen. In addition to some koans from outside the standard collections, I had in my interviews in the Poisonous Wolf's Cave gone through the whole hundred of the *Hekiganshu* and got up to number 37 of the *Mumonkan* classic.

When I received the red-coloured conscription papers, I went at once to see the Roshi at Tenchian hermitage at

Kuboyama, and told him the position. Saying "Oh, really?" he got up from his seat and went into an interior room. He soon came back with two sheets of coloured paper about a foot square, on which he had brushed:

No life-and-death for this one
Indomitable courage

The first comes from a phrase of the founder of Myoshinji in Kyoto, the great Kanzan, one of whose names was Egen: "No life-and-death for this Egen."

These two sheets of paper with their brushed characters were always with me during my army service, and later when we were all imprisoned in Russia.

When I was called up, I was engaged on the 38th koan in the *Mumonkan*, which is Ho-en's "Cow Passing the Empty Window." When I said farewell to Master Gyodo I asked him, "How would it be if I try writing my solution to you?" "Interview by letter?" he said doubtfully, putting his head a little to one side. "Well, you could try it," he then agreed. I did in fact write from where I was stationed two or three times, to have the Zen interview on paper as it were, but after that I gave it up altogether. I was assigned to an anti-aircraft unit and we were immediately sent to the barracks at Shimamatsu in Hokkaido. We were engaged in the defense of the air above Otaru City. In May 1943 we were ordered to two of the northernmost islands of the Kurile chain. The small mountains rising in the middle of the islands were covered with snow year round. From one of them, Kabuto-yama, on a fine day I could get a distant view of the snow-white peninsula of Kamchatka, and realised how far north I had come.

On these North Kurile islands there are many days of dense fog in summer, and raging snowstorms in winter. The fog is famous for its peculiar humidity, which sometimes made our clothes as wet as if they had been soaked in water. The snow-storms were so violent that they claimed several victims each winter. When one was raging, it required extraordinary care to traverse even the ten-odd yards which separated one of the barrack buildings from the next one. In addition to all this, the islands are subject to hurricanes, which not seldom attain a wind-speed of over 120 miles an hour.

The islands are quite barren, yielding no grains and hardly any vegetables. Food and other necessities of life had to be supplied to us by sea from Japan proper. Thus there were no actual inhabitants of the islands who lived there all the time.

All these circumstances combined to induce in one a feeling of deep desolation, as of being (like so many characters in Japanese history) exiled to a remote island surrounded by the ocean. Of course the arrival of a supply ship was a tremendous event. But these ships were from time to time sunk by enemy submarines. Raids by the American Air Force were very frequent. Soon after our arrival the barrack of a platoon of the searchlight battalion was hit by a bomb, killing not only its leader but the commander of the battalion and the men of a company who happened to be on the spot.

In this grim situation, however, it was still possible for me to study and meditate, by day and by night, whenever it was that I could get the time off from my duties. As for reading, I spent many days on Shimazaki's *Before Dawn* and Goethe's *Faust*. I borrowed the *Lotus Sutra*, translated from the Chinese, from an officer in the paymasters department, and read it over twice with great spiritual benefit. If the *Record of Rinzai* is comparable to a serene gem, the *Lotus Sutra* is a magnificent temple decorated with innumerable precious stones. I was also stirred by the proselytizing spirit pervading this sacred book.

After I had read it for the second time, I happened to hear that a man in a certain company had a copy of the Chinese version, and when I next went to that company, following the regimental commander on an inspection tour, I took the opportunity to borrow the book. I copied selections from the twenty-eight chapters of it, in tiny characters in a pocket book; a few of the chapters I copied out in their entirety. I also wrote those passages which impressed me most as the essence of the Lotus Sutra on some small sheets of paper.

Our arrival in the North Kuriles took place immediately after the annihilation of the Yamazaki garrison on Attu in the Aleutian islands in May 1943. After that, the tide of war had been steadily turning against Japan, and it was expected that there might be American landings on our islands any day. We were given preparatory exercises for a final battle in which all were to die in action, with no one surrendering. The exercises in hand-to-hand fighting, officers with swords and men with bayonets, were repeated again and again.

Surrounded by such an atmosphere of grim desperation, I read and meditated as before, but also took up daily sword practice with a wooden practice sword or my real one. Before being called up, I had a little instruction in an ancient tradition called *batto-jutsu*, the art of drawing a sword and striking with a single rapid movement. This is one of the sources of the developed Japanese art of the sword, and I took up the practice again. Among the books I had brought with me was Miyamoto Musashi's *Five Rings*, which I now studied with profit.

After reading the chapter on "How to Use the Feet and How to Walk," I happened to pass a dried-up riverbed full of boulders. Going down to the bed I drew my sword and struck out in all directions against imaginary opponents, at the same time having to keep my balance and freedom of movement among the stones. This experiment brought home to me the real value of Musashi's teachings.

In the chapter on "Sight in the Knightly Arts," it is said:

Of pure awareness and the physical eye, it is very important in the knightly arts that all-seeing, imperturbable awareness should be the stronger of the two, so that one should be able to see the distant like the near, and the near like the distant. It is most important in the knightly arts to know your opponent's sword, without looking at it at all. You must try hard to learn how to do so... It is also important to see either side without moving your pupils to the side at all. If you are taken up with the world, you cannot expect to learn the secret in a short time. Take to heart what I have written here, and always practise fixing the gaze in this way, so that it does not waver. This has to be wrestled with again and again. This is in the *Book of Water*.

The last section, called "Emptiness," has this:

You should diligently cultivate the spirit and the mind, as well as awareness and the physical eye, every day and every hour. When you have made them cloudless and free from all delusions, then you may be sure that you have attained the spiritual state of true 'Emptiness.'

From this it is clear how much importance Musashi attached to the point about awareness and the physical eye. This having taken a firm hold of my mind, I exercised myself in it with my sword every day, in a little wood of alders (dwarfed by the cold), and against the background of the mountains clad with perpetual snow. On the 16th of July, 1944, when I was training myself in awareness and physical eye along these lines, with the bare sword before me, I realised the real meaning of the phrase: "Cold stands the sword against the sky," and I saw that I had never really understood it.

At the same time I had a realization of knowing from the inside the first koan of the *Hekiganshu* (Blue Cliff Record): "Vastness, no holiness!", and the comment in the Gateless Gate (No. 19): "When you attain the way of no doubts at all, it is an abode of vastness like infinite space," and Shido Bunan's state of "Nothing to Defend," and again the poem which the fencer Yamaoka Tesshu composed on his enlightenment: "One morning the floor and walls were all pulverised and I saw the round dewdrops shining as ever." (The passage in Bunan's work *The Heart As It Is* runs: "Someone asked me about Mahayana, and I said, 'Keeping oneself upright, to have nothing to defend, that is Mahayana.' Then he asked about the highest Way, and I said, 'Doing just as one likes, to have nothing to defend, that is the great thing. And that is why there are very few such in the world."')

I returned straightaway to my room and went right through the hundred koans of the Blue Cliff and the first thirty-seven of the Gateless Gate, one after another. I had already passed through each of them in the interview room with Master Gyodo, but now I felt that I had penetrated into their very marrow.

I came to see how significant was the "Vastness, no holiness!" koan at the very beginning of the Blue Cliff. Vastness. Great Emptiness. Empty Space. Nothing to Defend, express the Dropping off Body-mind, Bodymind dropped-off state which is the essence of Zen, and the marrow of all the classical koans.

I felt I had realised the state of which it is said "to pass one is to pass all" and "cutting through all the old koans." Since the time of first seeing the nature in November 1936, some eight long years had gone by up to this moment, with great changes in the situation of Japan and of course my own personal situation too. But this day was one of the most unforgettable of my whole life.

Years later, when in a priest's robe I was practicing the austerity of a mendicant in the streets of Kyoto, I looked in at the museum and chanced upon the admonition of National Master Daito, in which he says, "The Great Teacher Bodhidharma came from India across the turbulent waves, and saw first the Liang lord (the emperor Lang Wutei) to whom he declared 'Vastness, No Holiness!' The thousand miles and ten thousand miles were like one bar of iron. After that he went to Shaolin, and there was the test of his four disciples who grasped skin, flesh, bone, and marrow respectively. All was nothing more than 'Vastness, No Holiness!'... " Reading this closely, I felt it was a confirmation of my experience in the Kuriles in July 1944.

Back in Japan after being a prisoner in Russia, I one day spoke of this realization in the Kuriles to Master Gyodo, who listened in silence. Then he just said: "However good a thing may be, it will not do to get caught up in it." Gyodo Roshi always admonished us strictly: "Don't get caught up in anything at all. Go beyond everything!"

I heard the Emperor's broadcast on Horomushiro island announcing the cessation of hostilities, and toward the end of August 1945 we were taken prisoner by the Soviet Army. We were put together with other units in large warehouses near the airstrip, and in this very anxious and restrictive situation we each had to get on with our lives as best we could. I used to go into the trees every day and chant the *Kannon Sutra* and the *Essence of the Lotus Sutra* which I had compiled in a loud voice. Then one day I was asked by the regimental commander to give a talk on zazen (contemplation) to an audience of nearly all the officers, after which, gradually, they began to sit together most evenings for a short time before going to sleep. However, this did not last long, as in November we were put onto a Russian ship. We hoped we were going to be repatriated to Japan, but our hopes were dashed when the ship made for a Russian port.

December 8 – celebrated especially in Zen as the day of the Buddha's realization – was the day we docked at Vladivostock; and in the middle of the next night we were disembarked into the darkness and piercing cold. Carrying all our baggage, it was no easy matter just to keep going. Any upward slope seemed to make the packs heavier and the pain harder to bear. To breathe was painful, and at times it seemed that death was close at hand. Involuntarily and half-consciously I found myself reciting *"Namu Kannon bo-satsu"* (reverence to bodhisattva Kannon). Gritting our teeth, we somehow struggled on, with occasional warning shots fired by the guards into the air. Finally we stumbled into the primitive prison buildings.

We were held there two weeks, with appalling food consisting mainly of thin gruel. At night it was so crowded that our boots were in our neighbours' faces. If one went to the latrine during the night, on returning one found that the sleeping place had just vanished.

Doubtless owing to a constitutional weakness, I got frostbite on the face when walking in the tiny garden.

At the end of December we were packed into railway trucks, and for forty days we were on the trans-Siberian railway, until we ended up in a prison camp near a forest, in a plain not far from Moscow. In the trucks I got frostbite again, but one of us had such a serious case that he had to have a leg amputated. That was a terribly painful journey for us in the trucks, through the Siberian winter, when the temperature is seldom higher than ten degrees below zero.

A few days into the train journey, I looked back over my time in the army, well over four years. In my own regiment, a whole battalion had gone down in a torpedo attack, and many others had been killed in air raids. I had been fortunate enough to survive so far, but it would evidently not be easy to come through the cruel hardships of life as a prisoner. It seemed to me that Japan, after losing this war, would have no political or economic power, and the only contribution Japan could make to world culture would be in the field of Buddhism. Japan's fine arts might possibly be an internationally valuable asset to that end. I resolved then that if I should return, I would devote the remainder of my life to the cause of Buddhism. This is the highest value I had met in life, and I would willingly be engaged in minor duties in some mountain temple if that was what offered itself. I would have some regret at renouncing my three little ones, leaving them without the loving care of their father, but they would realise that I might easily have died like so many others during the war itself. "I do not begrudge my body or life for love of the Supreme Way," says the *Lotus Sutra*, and indeed, unless there are some who are really to put the meaning of this verse into practice, the Supreme Way might easily die out.

This resolution became firm in me, and I spent my time in the gloomy goods truck in sutra chanting and meditating. As I look back on it now, I feel that this resolve was what kept alive a glimmer of hope which enabled me to survive those prison conditions.

The trucks on the Siberian railway did not give us much room. In the middle was a stove and a toilet; in the fore and aft sections there were two "decks," one above the other, crowded with forty men sitting or lying. When at night we wanted to sleep, we were so packed that each man's legs were bound to be interfering with the sleep of someone else, and there were noisy scenes every night.

The wagons had no windows but there was a single opening in the middle which let in some sunlight. However, I discovered a small knothole in the wall beside my place, and through its half-inch diameter a tiny ray of light could creep in. By that, I could read the *Mumonkan* and the *Lotus Sutra*. I was still able to practise meditation for a short time every day.

During the whole time I was at the prison camp, I read the *Rinzai Roku*, the *Lotus Sutra*, the *Hekigan Roku*, and the *Triple Scripture of the Pure Land Sect*: the last two I borrowed from a man in another unit; I heard by chance that he had copies of them. Similarly I came to hear of a copy of Dogen's *Gakudo Yojinshu* (Advice to Students of Buddhism). Getting the loan of this, I copied it out in tiny letters into a small notebook. The barrack was not furnished with electricity, and there were only a couple of small oil lamps among a hundred men. So I had to do my reading at night beside one of them, and find a place at the window during the day, because even then the place was rather dim.

In the winter round Moscow, even in daytime the temperature can be more than thirty degrees below zero, and it is often twenty-five below. At such times we were let off work in the open air, and confined to our barracks.

When we got back from work on the farm, I would try to learn by heart the two poems "Shinjin Mei" (On Faith in the Heart) and "Shodoka" (Song of Realization of the Way), and sometimes I would recite them walking about the courtyard of the barrack in the cold air which was far below zero. I had a good memory in those days, and could manage to get through the whole long "Shodoka" poem.

As for daily life, I recalled the saying in the Zen monastery: Practise the Mirror *samadhi* for three years. So I tried this mental cultivation (of clear awareness like a mirror) during activity, and when walking to and from the place of work.

On the days when the temperature fell below minus twenty-five degrees and we were let off our work in the open air, we consequently had an extra holiday. On some such occasions, when walking about the camp courtyard, I often felt a sense of gratitude welling up in my heart. It may seem a strange thing to say, considering the very adverse situation we were in: the strict confinement, anxiety about the very uncertain future, with only the barest necessities of life, and no possibility of being able to do what one might wish. But it is a fact that on a number of different occasions I had this feeling of thankfulness rising in me. It was not gratitude for any particular thing, but a sort of diffuse happiness, like the light of dawn coming up in the midst of darkness. I suppose that at the root of these experiences was what had come from following the way of Zen.

During the imprisonment of two years and some months, I dreamed of my teacher Gyodo Roshi only once. I saw him in a large study, sitting at a desk with a book placed on it. He said to me: "I want to give you this book, but as yet it wouldn't be any good." I remember that in the dream I had looked for, and brought to give to the Master, a pair of sandals with white thongs. I had this dream in 1946 on the night of October 15, which is the traditionally observed anniversary of the death of the Third Zen Patriarch in China, Songtsan, who wrote the poem "Faith in the Heart." It was of course chance, but had deep meaning for me, as I was wholly determined to give my life to Buddhism, and with that resolve alone sustain myself in the sufferings of imprisonment.

Every morning I used to recall the verse of Master Menzan:

When heart is in accord with heart,
And remembering with every thought,
There is a meeting every day –
Regardless of presence or absence.

I turned toward the sky in the direction of my home country, and prayed for Master Gyodo Furukawa and for Dr. Kitaro Nishida (Japan's greatest philosopher). After we arrived in Russia, someone told me that Dr. Nishida died, but I had not believed it.

The first part of the imprisonment in Russia had been at Patema, a prison camp situated among forests and fields; the last half was in a camp near Moscow at a place called Marshansk. It was from this last that we were finally repatriated to Japan. Our Siberia-bound train pulled out of Marshansk station in 1947, again on October 15, the anniversary of Songtsan's death. It was no more than coincidence, but once more I could not help feeling that it was somehow a confirmation of my resolve to give my life to Buddhism as a priest. And so, we returned to Japan.

After the experience of profound enlightenment which I had on Horomushiro Island in the Kuriles, I had a secret notion that I should have nothing to fear from any of the classical koans. But when I resumed the interviews with Master Gyodo after my return, I discovered that it was no such simple matter. The very first one I was given, about the ox passing through the window (No. 38 in the *Mumonkan*) took me quite a number of days to pass through myself. At the same time, thanks to this koan, there was a marked advance in my grasp of enlightenment. Master once said that to hold people up is what a koan is for, and one should appreciate this.

Anyway, it made me humble again, and I assiduously worked at the training in the Poisonous Wolf's Cave interviews. In the end, I was passed through the whole training of the interview room, and one day in May, 1949, was given a traditional hermitage name (*shitsugo*): Fuko-an, which means "the Hermitage of the Cloth Drum."

Along with this I was presented with a verse by the Master:

To the Master of the Cloth Drum Hermitage
He has burst open the long night's dream of sentient being
Across the ocean of No Merit,
His ship of compassion rides proudly
Feeling and thinking at a loss,
Like a fool, like a dullard, in light and dark.

He also remarked to me: "You have got the dharma, so whatever you do, it's all right."

The 57th koan of the *Hekigan* collection is Joshu's: "You yokel!" And Setcho's verse on it concludes with the line: "A cloth drum is hanging from the eaves." One day the Master gave a sermon in the Engakuji hall on this line, and he said that of course a drum which is made by stretching a cloth across won't make a sound however much you hit it. So it's something quite useless. In human terms it means a fool, someone quite useless. And (he added) you have to become an absolute fool. "I say fool, but it doesn't mean just to be in the way as an ordinary fool. You have to be a really big fool."

In the *Hokyo Zammai* classic it says "to be able to keep living like a dullard, like a fool, is called the lord of lords" – and when it is said that the cloth drum is like a fool, this will mean that it is a state not easily attained.

Twenty-four years after my start on the Way of Zen, though my pace was slow and unremarkable, I reached a certain landmark. Meanwhile many great changes had taken place, and not only in my private life, due in part to the China Incident (1937–41) and World War II. Having finished my spiritual apprenticeship, I keenly felt that I was charged with a fresh responsibility: the mission to propagate Zen Buddhism. And to this end I considered whether I would not do well to enter the priesthood, shaving my hair and assuming the priest's black robe. The reading of the *Book of*

the Merits of a Priest in Dogen's Shobo Genzo (a collection of his Japanese writings on Zen Buddhism) and also of the Most Reverend Daio's *Final Advice* gave a big new impetus to my resolve. As I pondered the question intently, I read and reread these writings.

I consulted Dr. Daisetsu Suzuki about my plan. He did not encourage me, saying, "In my opinion you need not enter the priesthood. But I admit priesthood has a certain prestige attached to it." He had used the English word and being uncertain about the meaning of the word "prestige," I consulted an English dictionary afterwards, and found it signified "reputation, influence derived from past achievements, positions, etc.," but that the original French word meant "illusion" and "disillusion" as well as "trick" and "glamour." Taking it all in all, prestige seemed to be an ironical word.

In the extensive grounds of Engakuji, some well-to-do people had built homes on rented sites: among them was Mr. Mitsuo Ishii, a retired businessman who was an ex-president of the Japan Hypothec Bank. In his younger years he used to study Zen under Master Sokai, a former abbot of the monastery. He was friends with many famous priests, such as Soen Shaku, Toin Iida, Shizan Ashikaga, and Gempo Yamamoto, and was recognised as the greatest collector of Zen books. After I had decided to become a priest, I consulted Mr. Ishii about whom I should request to be the master priest in my ordination. My old master Gyodo Furukawa was then in retirement. Mr. Ishii recommended the Most Reverend Kendo Ueki of Unganji in Nasu, Tochigi prefecture, saying that as far as he knew, Master Kendo was a man of noblest character. I accepted his advice, and was given a letter of introduction.

In June, 1949, I started for the temple. It was situated on a mountain fourteen miles southeast of Nishi-Nasuno station on the main North-East railway. It had been founded by the Most Reverend Bukkoku (one of the disciples of Bukko, a Chinese priest, who also founded Engakuji). In his time, the temple was renowned as one of the two greatest Zen centres in the country, the other being the Sufukuji at Hakata, Kyushu, presided over by the Most Reverend Daio. Alighting from the train at Nishi-Nasuno Station, and taking a local line and then a bus, I came within half a mile of my destination. Then I walked along a mountain stream called Mumogawa, and arrived at Unganji. Its traditional "mountain name" was Tozan (East Mount), standing as it did on the midslope of a thick, wooded mountain. The noise of the torrent was likely to be mistaken for the sound of falling rain at night by strangers staying at the temple, so perfectly still were the surroundings of this temple.

One of my first impressions was of its cleanliness. The lavatories especially were kept so clean that they were shiny. I was first received by the Reverend Daikei Hayashi, present abbot, and then presented to Master Kendo Ueki. With permission I stayed here overnight, and explained to the ex-abbot all about my past and present. Despite the fact there were no female inhabitants, there was something mild and kindly in the atmosphere, in striking contrast with that of the average Zen temple where sternness alone would prevail. In this kindliness my heart felt at ease.

"The education you are now engaged in is an important matter as you know," the Master began, "and before complete renunciation of the world you will have to provide for the support of your wife and family. So you had better take your ordination without giving up your present profession for now." It was arranged that I should come again toward the end of August during the summer vacation, for the purpose of taking the robe.

Immediately before taking the rites of ordination, I was to copy out a pledge, following a set formula. It consists of several lines, but the contents could be summed up in one sentence. "I vow to devote myself to the propagation of the Way, sacrificing everything." There was no mention of studying or practising the Way oneself, but it stressed exclusively propagation of the religion. Remembering that the *Lotus Sutra* was informed with the spirit of propaganda, I was struck by the manifestation of the Mahayana spirit in this formula. It is sometimes said that pity and love are lacking in Zen, and that compared to Christianity, Buddhism is poor in the spirit of propagation. Be that as it may, I realised on this occasion that the backbone of Zen was to be found in the cultivation of souls.

My master Gyodo had often said, "The first duty of a priest is to spread the religion. But nowadays there are few of them who will exert themselves in this way." Now, as I was writing out my pledge, his regretful words came back to me with great force.

"The aspiration to *bodhi* (enlightenment) means the vow to save all sentient beings before one's own salvation, and to exert oneself accordingly. Whether one be a layperson or a priest, a dweller in heaven or a human being, whether one is in pain or pleasure, one should resolve immediately to take the vow: 'I will save others before myself.' However humble one may be in his social estate if he takes this vow, he becomes a teacher of beings in heaven and on earth. Even if one may be a girl of seven, one becomes a teacher of the four ranks of Buddhists. Whether male or female such a one is the loving father of all creatures. This is the supreme principle of Buddhism. When one has taken the vow, one may happen to be born in any of the Six States of Existence or in any of the species of living beings, but such an existence will provide opportunity to fulfil the great mission of the bodhisattva. Though one may have lived idly up till now one should hasten to take the vow while life yet remains."

The above is a quotation from the *Book of Vow and Salvation*, in the *Soto Kyokai Shushogi* (Rules of Salvation and Enlightenment of the Soto Sect of Zen). I have repeatedly read this passage since my youth, sometimes finding my eyes filling with tears as I did so. The enthusiasm welling up from this passage is the backbone of Mahayana Buddhism. Unless inspired with this burning spirit, one's study and practice of Zen cannot have the sincerity it should have.

The rules of Meditation (*zazengi*) begin with the following:

"The bodhisattva who desires to attain the supreme wisdom ought first of all to entertain boundless compassion, vowing to save all beings and giving up the egoistic desire for his personal salvation."

It is highly significant that this text, whose object is to give a detailed account of the physical and mental methods of meditation, should first of all emphasise the importance of pity and love for all beings.

It would not be going too far to say that shouldering the cross of the pains and sorrows of humanity is the true source of sincerity in Zen study and practice. Hence the old saying that the identification of one's own good with the good of others is the essence of the way of bodhisattvas.

Renunciation of the world is not because of pessimism or escapism, as is often wrongly supposed: on the contrary, it ought to be for the sake of ridding the world of its misery. The distinction between Hinayana and Mahayana consists in this: that the former seeks one's own salvation exclusively whereas the latter is bent upon that of all creatures.

Before one can benefit others, however, one must have the experience or consciousness of having saved himself. Thus one's own good should be promoted by the desire for the good of others. On the other hand, the good of others cannot be achieved without one's own good. Study, practice, and propagation form a trinity. On the eve of my ordination, I was continuously taken up with these thoughts.

Master Kendo Ueki bestowed on me a stole, a robe, and a begging bowl, as well as the formal priestly name Genyo. But in fact I had my lay-disciple name Somei registered as my priestly name with the ecclesiastical authorities, keeping Genyo as a sort of pen name.

So it was, then, that having first conceived a vague idea of becoming a priest when I was only twenty-two, I now actually became one after a long time, when I was two months into my forty-sixth year. Immediately after the ordination ceremony, I had an interview with Master Kendo, in the course of which I asked him what would be the most important thing in my life as a priest in the future. He thought a bit and then said: "The most important thing is to have as few desires as possible." He also advised me for the present to continue to live at my home and carry on with my teaching as a professor. Accordingly, I took the train back to my wife and family at Kamakura, and I remember saying to myself seriously on the journey, contemplating my changed appearance with the black robe and shaven head: "You must be careful not to slip into becoming a hypocrite!"

Having been ordained a priest at Unganji in Nasu, I was still with my family and teaching at Kanagawa University as before, though now in priest's robes and shaving my head every few days. So I was a member of the class referred to in the old Buddhist saying: "There are four kinds of monks, one of them being those who remain with their families physically, but live away from the world spiritually." Again, in the section called "Ways and Means" in the *Vimalakirti Nirdesa Sutra*, it says: "If you have the aspiration for Supreme Wisdom (*anuttara-samyak-sambodhi citta*) then you are monks." In this spirit I tried to think of myself as a monk, though living a layman's life, but somehow in the depths of my being, I felt uneasy.

Often I thought to myself that I really ought to dedicate myself wholly to Buddhism without regard to my wife and children, and that the suffering which this would bring could be taken as a high sacrifice before the altar of the Way. Sometimes I was on the verge of taking the step of renouncing home to take a monk's life in the literal as well as spiritual sense; but then I would be watching them in our shared daily life, and particularly when I listened to their peaceful breathing in the silence of the night, a wave of feeling for them would come over me and my half-formed resolve would quickly crumble away.

During these times of spiritual struggle, I used to keep a small notebook with me, to jot down my passing thoughts and feelings, in the hope that somehow it would help to organise my thinking. But from time to time my predicament flared up into inner agonies, and it seemed like the situation in the saying "...a sheer cliff-edge behind, and another cliff-edge in front," or like a mountain climber who suddenly finds that there is no way to go on up, and no way down either.

Early in December of that year, I happened to come across a piece in the paper about two parents, both in their thirties, who had thrown themselves, and their four children, overboard from a cross-channel steamer going between Aomori and Hakodate. Their tragedy had not arisen from economic straits; they had relatively expensive tickets, and in fact the report said they were quite well-to-do Yokohama residents. Perhaps this story affected me so much because the places were familiar: I knew the Tsugaru Strait where the suicide had taken place, and I had myself lived for years in Yokohama. Such family suicides were often reported in the press, and more and more I found myself asking what our Buddhist priests were doing to alleviate the spiritual misery that must have occasioned them. And that led immediately to the thought, 'What am I myself doing? Am I myself leading the life proper to a Buddhist priest?' The repeated self-examination and subsequent self-reproach were reinforcing my wavering determination to renounce my family ties altogether.

About now I got a letter from Daisetsu Suzuki in America saying that there was a certain American in New York who was running a Zen meditation hall there, and was intending to come to Japan soon; he had mentioned my name to him, and he now asked if I would see this man. As it happened, I was not able to meet him when he came briefly to Kamakura; he went on to stay in Kyoto, and I corresponded with him. Finally I did meet him in Kyoto, and we had several days of talks there.

One day he suggested to me that I should go to New York at some future date, when he would provide the basic necessities of living for me, and also for my family if I decided to live there as a monk without them. I felt my heart jump at this proposal, and made up my mind there and then to give up my worldly occupation of teaching, and also to live in isolation.

In 1950, on the eighth of April, which as it happens is the anniversary of the birth of the Buddha, I left my home dressed in my priest's robes, and got on the train for Kyoto. On the way, I composed this haiku poem:

Leaving behind wife and children,
I seek to live as a monk without home,

Passing through the green of barley fields.

But I could not banish from my inner eye the pathetic figures of my wife, with her poor health, and of my youngest daughter of seventeen. At the same time, I had some feeling of relief that the long inner struggle was over, and that I was now confronting my own destiny.

In Kyoto I was first given lodgings in a small temple near the Ryoanji, which is so famous for its austere rock garden, and later in a hermitage in the precincts of Daitokuji.

In this last, I had the responsibility for cleaning the interior of the building and the gardens. The old monk living in the hermitage gave me instruction in chanting sutras, and the rules and ways of life of a priest, while I also undertook some studies of the doctrines of Buddhism on my own.

I had intended to attend regular classes at one of the Buddhist universities in Kyoto, but I did not manage to carry out this part of my plan. However, I used to visit Dr. Shinichi Hisamatsu and Dr. Keiji Nishitani, professors at Kyoto University, and Abbot Daiko Yamazaki of Shokokuji, Abbot Shinken of Tofukuji, and Roshi Bunken who was in charge of the Myoshinji Meditation Hall, and some others. It was a joy to come into personal touch with such distinguished scholars and Zen masters. I also attended some sessions for study of the *Yuima Sutra* and the *Record of Rinzai*, held at the Institute for Research into the Science of Culture at Kyoto University.

I used to think in those days of the priest's robe and the stole as symbols of a life of renunciation, and moreover as outward expressions of inner joy at being at last able to fulfill my aspirations after so many difficulties. I walked through the streets of the old capital as it were proudly displaying myself as a priest in priest's robes. I invariably wore the stole round my neck, and the traditional wickerwork hat of the priest.

One day I was invited to attend a meeting of the study group of students belonging to Hanazono Gakuin University, which is maintained by the Rinzai Zen sect. There was a professor of the university presiding over the discussions. I was surprised at the scepticism about Zen, and the whole of the present-day priestly life. This was not long after July 1950, when the famous Kinkakuji (Golden Temple) had been deliberately set on fire and burned down by one of the disciples of the abbot there. It had been built in 1397 by Yoshimitsu, one of the Ashikaga shoguns, and was one of the cultural treasures of Japan. What surprised me still more was that some of the students seemed to be expressing some fellow-feeling with the criminal. Then some others began to talk about the irregular private life of the chief priest of a Zen temple, who was known to have trained for many years in Zen. A number of the students openly expressed doubts about the virtues of Buddhist meditation, and a priest's role in general.

I was asked to speak to these young men, and I told them about my past life and what I was doing now, out of veneration for the Buddha, the dharma, and the sangha, as Master Dogen says.

It was out of supreme devotion for Zen that I had given up my university professorship and my home life, and given myself up to religion at the relatively advanced age of forty-seven. I told them also that I took a great delight in wearing priest's robes, because like the red flag for the Marxists, they were symbols of Buddhism, and I would never appear in public without them. Whether my words had any lasting effect on them I do not know.

My stay in Kyoto for the purpose of getting training in the life of a priest had been arranged at the suggestion, and with the assistance, of the American whom I have mentioned. He conducted a meditation hall in New York and wanted me to come over to be the teacher there. It was proposed that a certain Zen master, under whom my American would-be benefactor had himself trained, would supervise my training as a novice priest. However, after a little contact with this master, I realised that there was something about him that did not quite satisfy me. Considering the future, I decided to cut short my relationship with him. I sent a letter to the American to express my thanks for his kindness so far, but to say that I no longer felt I could go on with the project. I wrote to my wife and family explaining the decision, and suggested that as no more money would now be coming from America there was no alternative but to dispose of the house in Kamakura, the proceeds of which would secure their livelihood for quite some time to come. I realised what a shock this would be to them, but there was no other way of tiding over the present difficulties.

I went back to Unganji, and explained things to Master Ueki Kendo, who fully appreciated the position. As I was packing up my things, there came the news of the outbreak of the Korean conflict. This was a great anxiety to everyone, as it seemed very likely to presage another world war.

At this time of crisis I pondered within myself that what the world needed was souls to dedicate themselves to continuously praying for peace, leaving their own welfare entirely to chance. So I determined to live as a beggar myself, maintaining a continuous stream of prayer for the peace of the world. I returned to Kyoto with this decision, thinking that I might also be able to continue the study of Buddhism, which would surely be useful in furtherance of my mission in helping its propagation. I wrote a detailed letter to Master Ueki Kendo explaining what I intended to do, and others to my family, entreating them to try to understand.

So it was that from the middle of July I found myself walking the streets of Kyoto as a mendicant begging for alms. At each door I used to stand and chant the traditional *Avalokiteshvara Sutra* in Ten Verses. I did not want to seem to be too importunate, so instead of facing the door directly I stood sideways on, looking along the street as it were.

To beg for alms was quite a new experience for me, and it needed a great effort to overcome a sort of embarrassment in doing it: it was a bit like jumping off a cliff. The evening before my first day as a beggar, I had placed the mendicant's scrip in front of the Buddha shrine and chanted the *Hannya Rishubun* (*Arya-Prajnaparamita-naya-satapanca-sutika*) and others for hours, praying for blessings on my undertaking which would begin next day. In my beggar's scrip I put a copy of the *Zen-sect Scriptures for Daily Use* (a sort of Zen breviary), the *Lotus Sutra*, and the Christian Bible. I wanted to face the austerity armed with these sacred books.

The first day of my life as a mendicant was one of violent wind and rain. I had a raincoat made of thick oiled paper, and went on from door to door chanting the *Avalokiteshvara Sutra*, and tinkling my little bell, braving the curious or contemptuous stares of the general public.

I knew about the "emptiness of the three elements of gift," which is taught as the true spirit of the monk's begging. The three elements are: the giver, the receiver, and the thing given, and their emptiness or nonexistence should be realised in the mendicant's mind at the moment that he receives the alms. In actual practice, however, a monk does tend to notice one or other of the elements, and it is incumbent on him to cease to notice them by exercising mental control. I used to concentrate on the chanting of the sutra, and this became my method of practicing the emptiness of the three elements.

In July and August it is mostly boiling hot in Kyoto. My whole body used to get drenched with perspiration, and I could feel a burning heat on the soles of my feet through the thin straw sandals that were all that covered them. Through these not very favourable circumstances, I pursued my vocation of begging for alms. But at the end of the day, when I looked toward the hills of Mount Hiei in the east, it seemed to me that never had I seen them looking so beautiful and refreshing. Then again, as I became used to the routine, I began to feel a sort of inner serenity as I began my first chanting in the intended round of the day.

The income from my begging was very small. I still remember, however, some of the charitable people I met:

a high-school boy who when he saw me would stop and get off his bicycle to give me some small coins; a young girl who crossed the street for the same purpose; an elderly man putting his palms together in reverent salutation after making his gift; and once an old woman, on her way home from collecting her ration of rice from the distribution station, who came up and gave me some of it. I had not expected that in the poor quarters of the north of the city the people were in fact more generous than the inhabitants of houses in the richer parts. I remember going along one of those streets, and nearly all the houses had their front door shut. I went down the street chanting in front of each door, but no one ever came out. I recall the feeling of rejection, as if one had been somehow condemned, or had had a bucket of dirty water thrown over me. But as I went on with the sutra I recovered from this wave of heart-questioning, and was soon walking on confidently as before. The thought came to me: 'I worship the Buddha in every person: if I am fed, it is by the Buddha in those that feed me; I do not need to abase myself before any person. I do not demean myself before any person.' It was in those days that I learned to speak openly and listen wholeheartedly even to people I was meeting for the first time, provided they had a kindly attitude. I could accept hospitality in a calm state of mind. I was learning something of the freedom of the life of a priest, and I got a glimpse of the carefree heart of the renunciate poet-monk Ryokan.

In this way of life, however, I have to confess that I could not altogether free myself from attraction toward the other sex. Admirer of the ideal of chastity as I was, I was forced to recognise the irrepressible force of the sexual instinct in human nature. This recalled to me something said by one of the outstanding Zen masters of the relatively recent past in Japan, namely Shido Bunan. When he was seventy years of age, he wrote: "No priest or monk should approach a woman. Even though he does not infringe the precept, he cannot prevent his mind being affected by her presence. To approach a woman therefore is to initiate a karmic tendency toward the animal state. I make it my practice to avoid women because I am conscious of the residue of animal nature in my self."

Sometimes I would picture to myself how pleasant it would be if only I could afford to have my wife come and live with me here in Kyoto. But I had barely enough to live on myself, and to support a wife, and family as well, was quite out of the question. In one of the letters from Dr. Suzuki Daisetsu, then a professor at Columbia University, New York, he said: "Mendicancy is all very well, but can you not devise some modern substitute for the traditional way?" and Dr. Hisamatsu Shinichi remarked to me in Kyoto: "There are many Zen masters of the traditional type. I have a hope that you could become one of quite a different type," and he added that there was a need of a Zen master who renounced not only the layman's life but also that of a priest.

As time went on, I became aware of the growing weakness of my body. Master Gyodo sent me a word of advice: "In your present physical condition, it would be risky to continue like this through the severe Kyoto winter." Master Kendo wrote to me to return to his temple at once, for the sake of my health. These words from revered teachers were reinforced by my own realization that to persist with the present way of life would lead to total collapse.

My only object in renouncing layman's life had been to propagate the true Way which I had learned from my master, and the life I had adopted in Kyoto had been a means towards that objective. I thought to myself that it would not be reasonable to cling to the means at the expense of the final purpose.

So I went back to Kamakura, sold the house at Hase, and found lodging for my wife and the children at Obai-in retreat in the grounds of Engakuji at Kamakura. Then I returned to Unganji. This was in January 1951, and concluded my mendicant's life. But the lessons I had learned from it, namely inner freedom and serenity, remained with me as foundation stones for the future.

THE ZEN LIFE-STYLE OF REVEREND KENDO AT UNGANJI

The Unganji (Temple of Clouds and Rocks) is about fourteen miles southeast of Nishi-Nasuno station on the North-East line, in the mountains of Tochigi prefecture. Bukkoku Kokushi founded it as a Buddhist temple in the twelfth century, when Zen had barely reached Japan. Muso Kokushi, one of his followers, was for some time abbot of Unganji. A great survey was made by Sekiguchi Tai of all the places in Japan associated with Muso's life, and he commented that for beauty of natural surroundings, Unganji was one of the three most supremely impressive that he had seen. The temple grounds include some well-wooded hills covering some four thousand square kilometres, which was a bequest in the original grant of land for the temple. When I was there, the abbot was the Reverend Hayashi Taikei, the 59th in the line of succession.

The 58th abbot had been the old Zen master Ueki Kendo, who had given the ordination rites to me. When he had first come to live in the temple, he found some of the buildings in a state of advanced dilapidation. For instance, even the reception room next to the entrance to the priests' living quarters had no sliding doors at all, and there were not enough of the trays and standard low tables for the monks to sit for meals and take their soup and rice gruel. It took him ten years of great efforts before the temple was restored to a sound financial condition, so that he could rebuild the present Buddha Hall. As a matter of fact, being an enthusiast for public education, his original plan had been to use the saved-up money to build a middle school. But some of the supporters of the temple, who had generously contributed to the funds, pressed the case for a new Buddha Hall, and he acceded to their wishes.

For the ceremony of installing the Buddha images in the new Buddha Hall, my old master Gyodo, then abbot of Engakuji, was invited to preside. The Rinzai Zen sect in Japan has a number of sub-sects, one of which is called the Engakuji sect, because its headquarters, so to say, are at Engakuji. Unganji belongs to this Engakuji sect; in fact the founder of Engakuji, Bukko Kokushi, had been what one might call the honorary first Zen abbot of Unganji. This was in the thirteenth century, and he is not to be confused with Bukkoku Kokushi, who had actually founded Unganji as a Buddhist temple in the previous century. This circumstance, seemingly so trivial,

I mention because it marked a remarkable coincidence in my own spiritual life. The personal name of Bukko Kokushi (which is a title meaning National Teacher Buddha-Light) was So-gen, and his pen name was Mugaku (Without Learning). When Master Kendo gave a new Buddhist name at an ordination, he made it his rule to make one of the syllables a *gen*, in memory of So-gen. In my case, the name chosen was Gen-yo, having the same *gen* syllable as the first one.

Master Kendo had been born in the township of Kaya, in Okayama prefecture, on September 15, 1871. He was the eighth son of Fujii Kyuemon, who combined farming and medical practice. He was ordained as a Buddhist novice by Soshun, priest of the local Saifukuji, on December 8, 1882. He was thus eleven years old, and he stayed at the temple until he was twenty-two. During this time he had some experience in teaching as an assistant at the nearby elementary school. In 1893 he went to Shofukuji at Kobe, where he entered the attached monastery. The next year he moved to the much bigger monastery at Myoshinji, the famous head temple of the Myoshinji sub-sect. For ten years, until 1903, he trained under Zen master Kokan there. When Kokan died, his successor Shozan continued the training, until he finally received the formal attestation as a Zen master himself.

The late Dr. Nishida Kitaro, whose philosophy was rooted in Zen, had been a disciple of Kokan, and was a close friend of Shozan. Speaking about those days, Kendo said that Dr. Nishida had been a man noted for complete sincerity.

Master Kendo told us that Master Kokan had been very austere and frugal in his style of life. For instance, though he was very fond of tofu bean-curd cakes, he would never buy more than one half-cake at a time; when radishes were in season, he gave strict orders to limit the amount that was to be purchased, though he liked them. In his long life of over eighty-seven years, Master Kendo never broke the ban on meat diet and sex indulgence to which he had vowed himself. In these respects and in the general austerity of his life, he surely owed a great deal to the influence of Kokan. He once remarked to me: "Compared to my master Kokan, I live a very indulgent life."

At every meal he still continued to use the simple lacquer bowls which are given to the novices, and after eating he carefully washed and cleaned them himself according to the monastery regulations. He washed his underclothes for himself, and mended them with needle and thread – it was quite impressive to see this octogenarian senior priest of high rank plying the needle. He would also clean the lavatory which he used. He rose at the same time as the young monks, in the small hours of the morning. To set an example to them in every way, he conformed minutely to all the monastery rules and regulations for conduct. On the wall in his room there was always a piece of paper with some motto for his own behaviour, just in the way that junior monks are encouraged to write up their own mottos.

Once when I was in his room helping him with some business papers, it began to get dark as evening came on, and I moved to turn on the light. He reproved me for wastefulness, saying: "It is still too early. There's enough light." I was impressed by his insistence on strict economy, and a phrase of the old master Shido Bunan came to my mind:

"We should be very careful in making use of a half-sheet of paper, or in spending a half-penny."

From time to time I was called to his room to write letters he dictated. Occasionally seeing that I was about to begin a new line, he would check me, saying: "You have still got some space at the end of the line." When writing postcards for him, it could sometimes happen that the card was full up with writing, but he wanted to add something extra. Then I would be told to use a fine pen, and write in red ink between the lines.

It might seem that such extreme economy is almost meanness, but in fact he would always give money gladly when there was some reason for it. When he had guests, he treated them most hospitably. He always impressed on the people at the temple: "Be kind to others!" and he followed the principle himself. He was all strictness about his own conduct, but generous in judging others, always seeking to look on the good side of everyone and shut his eyes to the bad side. He used to say: "When I consider my own failings, I find I cannot criticise others." When I was living at Unganji, my own behaviour was not always exactly what is traditional in a Zen disciple, but Master Kendo was patient and tolerant of my shortcomings. His warm-heartedness made me look up to him more and more as a sort of incarnation of Kannon, the bodhisattva of mercy.

He was always concerned about the troubles of those with whom he had contact, and he would willingly undertake the arduous journey to Tokyo from his remote temple on the Nasu plateau if he heard of any serious difficulties in their families. In fact we used to be careful in the evenings to see that he should not hear of any such thing that he might feel anxious over. For he used to take these troubles to himself, so that he would not sleep until, sometimes in the middle of the night, he had gotten up and written a letter to them. I once heard him mutter to himself: "It does make it awkward when I am rung up about a serious matter in the evening."

Still, this extreme kindliness of character was backed by a parallel trait of severity. According to one who had trained for some time at Unganji when the Master was in his fifties, Master Kendo would sometimes lose his temper when he came across some serious negligence on the part of a disciple. He remembered seeing the Master, brandishing the bamboo broom with which he had been sweeping the garden, running after a young monk and hitting him across the shoulders with it, as if it had been a *keisaku* (the warning-stick used in the meditation hall to arouse the slack).

From occasional remarks he made about his own training period at Myoshinji, I gathered that he had sometimes a disagreement with some senior monk about some point or other. At those times, if at the end of the argument he was still convinced of the rightness of his own position, he would never submit to their ruling.

Even in old age, when he got up in the morning he would lock his hands above his head, stretch them straight up vigorously above his head, and give a tremendous shout. It had an electrifying effect on those who heard it.

I came to the conclusion that the kindliness, which I as well as others experienced, was so to say the flesh on the bones of inner strictness and austerity.